Publications of the
CENTER FOR EDUCATION IN
INSTITUTE OF INTERNATIONA
Teachers College, Columbia University
David G. Scanlon and L. Gray Cowan, editors

Language, Schools, and Government in Cameroon
HUGH O. H. VERNON-JACKSON

Divergence in Educational Development: the Case of Kenya and Uganda
SHELDON G. WEEKS

Political Socialization in the New Nations of Africa
PENELOPE ROACH

Educating the Bureaucracy in a New Polity
TAMAR GOLAN

"Education for Self-Reliance" in Tanzania (A Study of Its Vocational Aspects)
WILLIAM A. DODD

The Development of Education in East Africa
JOHN CAMERON

The Cost of Learning: The Politics of Primary Education in Kenya
L. GRAY COWAN

The Cost
of Learning:

The Politics of Primary Education in Kenya

L. GRAY COWAN

Center for Education in Africa
Institute of International Studies
Teachers College, Columbia University

TEACHERS COLLEGE PRESS
Teachers College, Columbia University
New York, New York

Preface

In any country, regardless of its stage of development, the educational system is a matter of controversy. In the developing areas, the close relationship of educational attainment to a role in the modern world brings the content and extent of education into even sharper public focus and consequently makes it, to an even greater extent than elsewhere, a matter of political concern.

The present study seeks to emphasize the connection in Kenya between primary education and politics, in the context of local control through elected County Councils over this segment of the educational system.

Field research was undertaken in 1967 and 1968, although statistical material refers to 1966, the latest year for which relatively complete figures were available.

I am most grateful to my colleagues Professors Daniel Rogers, David Scanlon, and James Sheffield of Teachers College, Columbia University, for their valuable comments on various stages of the manuscript. I am indebted as well to Mr. John Anderson of the Department of Education of the University of East Africa, Nairobi, not only for his comments on the manuscript but for his guidance and help throughout the field research. I received invaluable assistance with background research and with the checking of facts from my research assistant, Miss Penelope Roach, and a special word of acknowledgment is due to Ronald L. Friesen for his assistance with statistical calculations.

My deepest gratitude should be expressed, however, to the many officials of the Kenyan Ministry of Education and the Provincial Administration, to the County Education Officers and to officers and members of the County Councils who everywhere gave unstintingly of their time and knowledge in hours of interviews. I can only hope that they will understand that my appreciation for their help is none the less profound because they remain anonymous. It is

v

customary, but perhaps superfluous, to add that mistakes of fact and sins of misinterpretation are entirely my own responsibility.

For assistance with field work I owe my warmest thanks to the Rockefeller Foundation, The School of International Affairs of Columbia University, and to the Program of International Studies at Teachers College.

October, 1969   L. G. C.

Contents

Introduction

The expansion of primary education has been a matter of utmost concern to the new governments of independent Africa almost from the point at which they assumed control over their own internal affairs. Education for the coming generation was regarded both by the political leadership and by the people as the key to entry into the world of modern technology. Without it the road to a better life, as symbolized by a role in the monetary economy, was closed. Parents everywhere in Africa were prepared to make personal sacrifices to educate their children, perhaps not always purely for the sake of the enrichment of the child; education was also a form of social insurance, to provide for the parents' old age, when they would be dependent on the earnings of their children.

Because the attainment of primary education was regarded as the first step up the new economic ladder, it became a matter of concern to the average man to a degree matched by few other post-independence issues. In Kenya, as elsewhere in Africa, the transfer of political control to an indigenous government paved the way for a popular demand for wider facilities in education, and nowhere was the demand more pressing than in the rural areas, which had been in close contact with the farmer-settler communities. The burden of those new facilities which were created fell directly on the parents who paid school fees, and while more and more parents paid higher fees gladly enough, they expected at the same time to be able to exert a measure of control over the expenditure. Primary education became a political issue of the first magnitude, and the budding politician who failed to take an acceptable stand on it found that his support was likely to evaporate. Primary education was a major preoccupation of local government, often to the exclusion of issues that had more than a just claim on the attention of the elected local representatives.

It may be cogently argued that the parents' concentration on formal primary education for their children was misplaced, and that the years spent on primary school education, which was designed to prepare its pupils for entry into the next higher level of education, would be of little value in preparing the child for life in a rural community. Such has proved to be the case for many of Kenya's school leavers, of whom only a little over 10 percent have been able to continue their education. It may well be that, from the point of view of the development specialist, resources that were devoted to raising the number of available rural schools might better have been used on projects of an infrastructural nature, or for other than formal educational services. Guy Hunter, in a recent monograph on Tanzanian rural education, emphasizes:

> The decisive shortage of educative effort does not lie, at the present moment, in the system of formal education. This may seem a quite extraordinary statement to make when over 45% of all Tanzanian children of school age cannot enter school for lack of recurrent income. But the vital fact is that some 46,000 young people in Tanzania completed seven or eight years of education in 1965, for the majority of whom no really productive activity can be found.[1]

Despite the evident truth of this point for Kenya, as well as Tanzania, an argument in this vein has a certain air of unreality about it, because it tends to ignore the popular pressures for increased educational facilities that simply cannot be ignored by those in political power at any level of government.

The present essay, which is part of a larger inquiry into local government and politics in Kenya, lays no claim to being a study in the technical aspects of educational or manpower planning. Rather, it is an attempt to look at the costs of primary education in terms of their effects on local government and on the relationships between local and central authorities. While most of these costs are in monetary terms, they extend beyond the realm of finances to political and social costs as well. The financial cost of primary education may well be more than local authorities can or should be called upon to bear, but their interest in retaining a voice in education must be balanced against the possible advantage of central government financing (and control) of the primary schools.

The issue of control over primary education in Kenya today raises and illustrates a number of broader questions that have implications for the general area of subnational political development. To a point, the interests of both local and national governments run parallel in education. Each is seeking to use the educational system as an instrument of development, but from the point of view of the center an equally important function of education is as a lever to promote national integration. Balanced educational development throughout the country may be one of the goals of national government, but the process of achieving it creates an inevitable clash with local interests, who see the expansion of education for their own children slowed down while other areas catch up. When national and local interests diverge too sharply on an issue of crucial importance such as this, the already somewhat tenuous links between national and local levels of the party organization become severely strained.

Control over primary education lies at the heart of the complex of issues centering around the penetration of the central government's powers into the rural areas. The content of the curriculum and the training of teachers remains, as it must, a function of the center while the financing of education is a local function. To maintain efficiency and adherence to its own regulations, the central Ministry of Education must have its technical representatives at the local level. Depending on the effectiveness of the local authority, the ministry's man inevitably exerts a degree of control often deeply resented by those with whom he must work. The presence of central authority is constantly felt, and just as constantly rejected as an alien intrusion into what is viewed as essentially a local concern. Yet the need for the technical advice provided by central authority is understood locally, and, so long as primary education requires central financial subsidy, there is little the local authorities can do but suffer, although by no means always in silence. On the other hand, central authority can only be pressed so far without the risk of popular repercussions that may threaten the political careers of the party's supporters in the legislature.

In the case of Kenya, center-local relationships are exacerbated by the presence, not only of representatives of technical ministries at the county level, but by the competing authority of the Provincial Administration, whose role looms increasingly larger as the local authorities begin to lose their financial independence through overexpenditure on primary education. As direct emanations of the power of the President, the Provincial and District Commissioners are a more solid link with the center than are the representatives of the Ministry of Local Government, who are, except for periodic visits, only in indirect contact with the County Councils. In theory, the members of the Provincial Administration are civil servants, but it became clear immediately preceding the abortive local government elections in August 1968 that the President regarded them as servants of the ruling party as well.

Symbolic of the deeper penetration of central authority into the shrinking autonomy of the County Councils was the government's recent decision to make the District Commissioner chairman of his council's powerful finance committee, replacing his former position as an ex-officio member of the council with the same voting rights as an ordinary member of the council. With few exceptions, counties and districts are conterminous, so that each County Council has a District Commissioner as a member. This new responsibility, combined with his existing dual responsibilities for law and order and local development (he is chairman of the development committee), permits the District Commissioner to override the council at almost every point. The justification for adding to his power is the necessity to protect the solvency of the council, but the net effect is to undermine the already eroded independence of the local authority.

It is difficult to counter the argument that greater efficiency in budgeting and expenditure can be achieved by central intervention in the affairs of the County Councils and that it is the duty of government to make sure that the taxpayer receives the fullest value for the revenue expended on education. Local authorities are not in a position to hire staff of the caliber employed by the central government. Moreover, where the question of the allocation of scarce resources must be raised, the central government may well be in the best position to make the most equitable distribution in the national interest.

But there is another side to the case, which in the long term may have equal or greater validity. Efficiency may be bought at the sacrifice of both flexibility and the ability to tailor an educational program to the specific development needs of an area. If all decision-making powers are effectively removed from the local authority, and if the impression is left that the individual is powerless to alter the decisions taken in any case, the reaction of the community may well be the gradual withdrawal of cooperation with the central authorities. In the rural areas, the values supposedly represented by efficient modern administrative practices may not necessarily be held in as high esteem as in the capital, and the basis for judging "good" government may rest on rather different assumptions. Professor Simon Ottenberg's comment on local government in Eastern Nigeria is largely applicable to Kenya:

> Today [as opposed to the colonial period] there is, in theory, separation of public and private interests, specifically defined governmental roles, and role interrelationships and universalistic recruitment of persons for office ... the members of the Town Council do not always clearly understand their place in the rapidly changing governmental scheme of things and by and large for them this is their first political office, a stepping stone for some to larger careers in politics. ... The underlying largely universalistic values of English local government have never really taken seed. ... Corruption, which occurs, ... may be seen as an adjustment to operating in a rational-legal bureaucratic structure in a traditionalistic manner.[2]

It might be added that, insofar as the local elected councils in Kenya are concerned, central supervision of finances has not, in the past, guaranteed against corruption. In part this has been due to the intermittent nature of the supervision, which may be remedied by the presence of the District Commissioner in a key financial post. Within broad limits, however, effective supervision can be exercised by the voters, who are more closely connected with the local situation and expect the council to maintain a certain level of services, especially in education. If the council falls below this acceptable level, members can be called to account often more effectively by local pressures than by a protracted legal process in the courts. To quote Professor Ottenberg again:

It is not a question that the British introduced a system of high morality which Nigerians could not accept, but that each system of authority has its own morality and rules of conduct which make for different views of the nature of governmental action and that in the absence of extremely strong checks by British or British trained persons (perhaps even if they were present), the more traditional forms of political action have come to dominate a structure geared to rational-legal authority patterns.[3]

Despite their shortcomings (which are shared by the local government bodies in many parts of Africa), the County Councils in Kenya provide a useful instrument of penetration for the central government, provided they can be persuaded to act in concert with the goals of the center. Apart from their value as potential sounding boards of public opinion, they take care of local administrative problems that would otherwise require the attention of high-salaried members of the central civil service. They provide, as well, a foundation upon which some services of government can be carried on whatever the disruptions that may be occasioned by sudden changes of leadership at the top. Finally, they provide opportunity for participation by the people at a level of governmental decision-making that is often more meaningful to the rural community than is the national level.

In return, however, if government expects the councils to be of service, they must be given a reasonable degree of control over significant areas of local interest. It cannot be expected that councilors of real ability will be content to spend their time over parish-pump politics. Primary education is one of those interests shared alike by the voters and councilors. To remove the powers over primary education would be to remove one of the major responsibilities of the councils, and would consequently substantially diminish their stature in the eyes of the voters.

But the interest of the central government in education is equally substantial and if the councils, in their eagerness to meet the demands of the public, overextend their capabilities, the center has little alternative but to curtail their activities. The dilemma is how to maintain that degree of control over the councils which will permit education to develop at a pace consonant with the absorptive capacity of the economy, and provide training that fits the product of the school for life in a rural area, without destroying the council's initiative. If the councils are deprived of their substantive powers over education, much of the popular interest in them as vehicles for the expression of local opinion will be dissipated, and their present and potential value, both politically and administratively, will be lost.

I

An Historical Overview
of Primary Education

From the outset of the period of colonial administration in Kenya, the financing of primary education has been a source of almost continuous controversy. It was the subject of numerous reports by official commissions and private individuals and groups, of innumerable memoranda within the administration, of debate in the Legislative Council, and of often bitter public discussion. Probably no subject except land has been more thoroughly and repetitiously gone into; unfortunately, in the case of education the discussion has led to less than substantial results.

It would be impossible here even to summarize the widely varying points of view that have been expressed; all that can be done is to indicate the outlines of the chief issues and of the attempts made to resolve them. For over half a century the responsibility for primary education has been tossed among the central government, the local authorities, and the missions. The administration repeatedly sought to free itself from the burden by leaving it to the other two groups, but, just as often in the past as today, political pressures for more rapid expansion of facilities have forced a return to the center when enthusiasm for education outran the ability to pay for it.

The content and direction of primary education has been affected from the beginning by controversy over its objectives. Even with the comparatively slow rate of African economic development in the early years, it soon became clear that the official view that education should be a strictly utilitarian outgrowth of an apprenticeship system had to give way to "literary education," as the demand for African clerks grew in the European business community. Primary education was caught up in the evangelizing zeal of the missionaries, leading eventually to the break away from the churches that gave rise to the independent-schools movement.

1

Little or no official attention was paid to education in the early years of British occupation. Until 1911 it was almost exclusively in mission hands, and tended to be concentrated around the major mission stations along the coast and around the lake. With the establishment of an Education Department in 1911, government control over education was exercised by the administration, and support for mission efforts came from public funds. Grants, at first for apprentices, then, by 1918, for "literary education," were provided, although on a minimal basis. The first Education Ordinance, passed in 1924, established a central advisory committee on education and school area committees on which the Local Native Councils (created in the same year) were to be represented. The councils contributed to education in their areas at a fixed rate of 2 shillings per taxpayer, only a small part of the real cost.

It gradually came to be accepted that responsibility for primary education should rest in local hands. In 1931 a new Education Ordinance gave the school committee power to advise the central education authorities on the use of funds provided by the Local Native Councils. The committees never functioned, however, in the manner hoped of them; they failed to act as the link between the community and the schools, in part because they lacked any real executive function. By 1934 they were replaced by District Education Boards (DEBs) with wider powers, which were concerned with day-to-day operation of the schools and on which the Local Native Councils and the voluntary agencies were represented. The boards were appointed slowly, however, in the rural areas and it was not until after 1951 that they generally assumed extensive powers over local financing of education.

The administration was reluctantly pushed into constant expansion of allocations for education, although the pace was seriously retarded by the depression years. But the burden fell even more heavily on the Local Native Councils. It was pointed out in 1936 that

> The cost to the Colony . . . in Government primary schools varies from £ 20 . . . to £ 12 [per pupil] . These figures exclude boarding expenses amounting to about £ 4 which are met by the Local Native Councils. Even in Mission schools the cost per pupil to Government varies generally from £ 16 to £ 12. . . . Obviously there can be no wide extension of primary education along these lines. . . . The two main reasons for the heavy expenditure are (1) that primary schools are boarding schools and (2) that high rate of salary paid to European teachers. . . . So far as native education is concerned the fundamental defect of the present position is that facilities for training teachers are utterly inadequate. . . .[1]

The primary schools referred to in this comment are what would under the present system be Standards IV through VII. They were at that time preceded by a five-year elementary cycle, consisting of two years subelementary and three years elementary.

The press for new education facilities continued, however, and despite government efforts at control, unaided schools sprang up everywhere. After struggling with the problem during the war years, the administration sought to reduce the financial pressure by refusing to increase the list of unaided schools unless the educational expenditures of a council did not exceed a specified formula. But the cost of teachers' salaries and of building continued to rise, and the ability of the missions to increase their donations fell until a crisis point was reached in the immediate postwar years. The publication in 1948 of the Ten Year Plan for the Development of African Education[2] further accented the problem with its recommendation that local expenditure for education rise from £ 100,000 in 1948 to £ 234,000 in 1957. The plan also clearly indicated that primary education should become the complete responsibility of local government. The structure of the system was redefined at this point to eliminate the former elementary grades, making primary school a six-year cycle beginning with Standard I.

The period of financial stringency with the onset of the depression of 1929 saw also the deterioration of relations between the mission groups who managed the bulk of the schools and the mass of Kenyan Africans. The growing cultural nationalism, especially in Kikuyu areas, could not fail to involve the educational process. Symbolized by the increasingly violent dispute over female circumcision between groups within the Kikuyu Central Association and the missions, a dispute that came to a head in 1928, suspicion of mission motives in education and the desire for African control finally brought about the emergence of an independent-schools movement. This was embodied in the Kikuyu Karing'a schools, which were later to be associated with the African Orthodox Church, and the Kikuyu Independent Schools Association (KISA), which was a predecessor of the Independent Pentecostal Church.[3]

The first African independent school was begun as early as 1925 at Githunguri. These independent schools were unaided; they were financed entirely from voluntary contributions by the people and were managed by local committees selected by the community.[4] The movement grew rapidly; specific figures on numbers of schools scarcely exist, but it is indicative that in 1937 fifty-four schools, with 7,223 pupils, were officially registered, ten of which were Karing'a schools. It is estimated by one participant in the movement that over four hundred schools were created, with an enrollment of more than 62,000 children. Probably there were many more, in more remote areas, that were taught by untrained teachers and did not reach the Education Department's standards or its attention. Applications were received in 1937 to open thirty-eight new schools the following year, despite a very severe shortage of teachers. Government policy was not to consider new schools until existing ones had been made more efficient, but official comment is significant: "It is hard to treat these new applications seriously except in the light of a political move. Nevertheless it is an indication of the strength of the movement."[5]

The evidence collected by the Beecher Commission in 1949 throws light on the attitudes of Africans toward missionary education and on the extent of the cash contributions that were forthcoming from the parents of children in these schools:

Table 1

Cash Contributions to Unaided Schools (1949)

	Total sh.	Contribution per pupil sh.	cts.
Kikuyu Independent Schools Association (Fort Hall)	44,685	44	00
Kikuyu Karing'a Education Association (Kiambu)	10,000	4	35
Kikuyu Independent Schools Association (Kiambu)	26,028	7	00
Kikuyu Independent Schools Association (Nyeri)	91,324	20	00
Holy Ghost Mission (Machakos)	650		25
Holy Ghost Mission (Kiambu)	3,125	1	35
African Christian Church and Schools Committee (Fort Hall)	10,110	10	00
African Anglican Church (Fort Hall)	32,388	10	00
Consolata Catholic Mission (Nyeri)	5,747	2	60
Consolata Catholic Mission (Embu)	4,529	4	00
Seventh Day Adventist Mission (So. Nyanza)	25,957	4	50
Mill Hill Catholic Mission (No. Nyanza)	3,794		50

Note: It is probable that the diversity in the figures contained in the last column of this table is, at least in part, due to the absence of careful records in some of the schools concerned, and to varying interpretations of the questions in the questionnaire sent out by the Committee.

Source: The Beecher Report, *African Education in Kenya* (Nairobi: Government Printer, 1949), p. 29 (Table X).

The commission's report points up African opinion on the education question in these terms:

African witnesses indicated they regard education as basic to all progress; they therefore had no hesitation in urging that there should be what they frankly recognize as unbalanced expenditure by African District Councils [the successors to the Local Native Councils] on education in relation to the other services for which these Councils are responsible. They further urged that payment for such an expanded educational service should be made by increased rates other than by increased fees for education; in support of this they urged that to do so spreads education costs over the whole community.[6]

However, the witnesses were emphatic in their desire to see results for heavier taxes in the form of more schools and to have African members of boards of management and school committees, particularly of the voluntary agencies (i.e., missions), so that full knowledge of how taxes were spent would be available.

African criticism of the missions centered around the tendency to give preference in schools to adherents of the churches that managed them, the fact that several schools often operated in one area because of denominational rivalries, overrigidity of mission discipline, and the failure of the missions to provide sufficient numbers of trained European teachers. Moreover, the missions were regarded by many as a barrier between the people and government behind which the administration took refuge in the face of popular insistence on greater facilities.[7]

African teachers in the mission schools were often the severest critics. In their evangelical zeal, the missions exerted a close and often suffocating control over the personal lives of their teachers to the point of risking open rebellion among them. One now famous former teacher has declared:

> I liked neither the flattery nor the underhand dealings with the staff. We were supposed to be government servants posted to work in missionary centers but our terms of service were not satisfactory compared to those who were fully in government service. I was disillusioned about the treatment of Africans by whites in the mission services.[8]

Much of the African criticism was undoubtedly justified; not a few of the missionaries saw education as a deflection from their true goal, evangelization. Mismanagement and lack of supervision of untrained teachers was all too common, as the observations of the administration attest. But the basic objection by 1949 was political. There was (and for that matter still is) suspicion that the missions were collaborating with the European administration to resist advances in African control of African education, and were acting as brakes to African economic progress.[9] At the same time, however, it was admitted that without the missions education would have been much less widespread and substantially more costly.

It was not accidental, of course, that much of the bitterness toward the missions was concentrated in Kikuyu territory. Not only was there a struggle going on to preserve Kikuyu custom against missionary encroachment, but from the earliest period the Kikuyu had clearly seen the advantages of the wider spread of education. As early as 1928 it was reported that Kikuyu Province had received nearly one half of the total allocation of grants in aid for African education (£ 12,332). The Local Native Councils "showed themselves eager to further education of their people. . . . Kikuyu Councils have resolved to spend more than £ 20,000 on education. This sum has been voted by districts and district loyalty is being fostered. . . . Apart from three schools in Fort Hall District under government control, all the Kikuyu schools are mission schools."[10]

In the following year, the Education Department concluded in some alarm:

> The dominating factor in the situation is the demand of the African himself for the provision of educational facilities through other than missionary agencies. The native of Kenya especially in the Kavirondo districts and in the Kikuyu Province has indicated in no uncertain terms his wish to be educated in institutions which are not under the care of missionaries.[11]

This sentiment was re-echoed many times over the following thirty years, but the missionaries remained a vital cog in the educational machine up to the point of independence.

The Ten Year Plan and the Beecher Commission Report brought some order to educational planning in Kenya, but the following decade was to show how greatly both documents underestimated the eventual expansion of primary education. The commission expressed itself as "satisfied that the provision which we propose will be found adequate to present needs and to those of the foreseeable future without the necessity for opening schools outside the plan."[12] It was estimated that by 1954 primary education would cost £ 429,000, of which £ 236,000 would come from local authorities and £ 193,000 as subvention from the central government. In fact, by 1954 the District Education Boards were controlling an expenditure of £ 1,230,297, of which the African District Councils paid £ 312,918 and the central government £ 568,289, the remainder being made up from school fees.[13]

The Work of the District Education Boards

The DEBs, whose continuation was recommended by the Beecher Commission, had proved since their inception to be useful instruments for the administration of education. There was some demand that the Local Native Councils themselves should become the education authorities, but they were already adequately represented on the boards, and the boards had for the most part been willing to comply with the councils' demands for more schools. To meet the objection that the voluntary agencies were too heavily represented in the original composition of the boards, they were reconstituted under the Education Act of 1951 to include the District Officer as chairman, the District Education Officer (DEO) as secretary and executive officer, and four representatives each of the Local Native Council and of the voluntary agencies. The boards were empowered to prepare estimates for submission to the council and to the Director of Education, to receive subventions from government and the local authorities for the purpose of paying grant-in-aid money to the voluntary agencies, and to plan for new school development. In general terms, they were to be the link between the central government and local education in order to keep the Director of Education informed on progress. The DEBs were empowered to invite to assist them, as nonvoting members, individuals whose special interest was education.

Boards were gradually appointed within the jurisdiction of each local authority, including the counties and municipalities that were the chief areas of European settlement. By 1961 thirty-six boards had come into existence, overseeing more than five thousand schools throughout the country.

It should be emphasized that the administration did not intend the DEBs to be representative or executive bodies. They were advisory, designed to give the local community some means of expressing an opinion on educational issues, but appointments to the boards were made by the Minister of Education at his pleasure. As the administration changed from the colonial structure toward self-government, the role of the Director of Education was assumed by the Minister. Moreover, since their executive officer, the District Education Officer, was a civil servant, there was little likelihood that he would permit the board to advise action that might conflict directly with government policy on education.

The schools supervised by the DEBs were financed in part from central government and in part from local revenue sources. In the case of the counties and municipalities (which at that time consisted entirely of units of local government within the European settler community), government grants to the boards covered 100 percent of the approved estimated expenditure on education. African education, on the other hand, was partially financed by grants from the African District Councils (ADCs). According to a formula devised by Sir Ernest Vesey, a former Minister of Finance, the central government provided a grant equal to double the contribution made by the ADC. The council itself was used as the channel for transmission of the grant to the DEB, which used the funds to defray the costs of operation of schools (chiefly tuition) over and above the fees paid by the parents. The council's contribution came from the flat-rate poll tax (varying in 1962 between 20 and 60 shillings, depending on the area) levied on its African taxpayers.

Examination of expenditures by the ADCs over representative years from 1954 until independence shows that their major financial burden was in education. Between 1954 and 1959, education budgets for the councils rose from a total of £ 407,821 to £ 1,831,970, of which £ 703,171 fell directly on the councils.[14] Almost 50 percent of the total expenditure by ADCs in 1959 (£ 3,997,669), can be accounted for by education alone. Over a two-year average (1959-61), central government education grants totaled only 31.4 percent of the income of all ADCs.[15] The high expenditure on education is scarcely surprising, of course, since popular interest in education, as the independent-schools movement amply illustrated, was of long standing; indeed, as one official commented, "the councillors themselves, if given free reign, would spend money on education to the detriment of other services such as health, water supplies, etc."[16]

There is no doubt that the Vesey formula gave considerable impetus to educational expansion. Some councils, such as Nyeri, were spending 10.6 shillings per capita on education as compared to 2.4 shillings on health and sanitation. But the 2:3 matching system had within it potentially serious long-term consequences in that it tended to reinforce the already evident differences between the rates of development of richer and poorer areas of the country. Those councils which through greater prosperity were able to raise higher sums in poll rates, and which were prepared to devote more to education, were at a distinct advantage under a fixed rate formula. So long as it was possible for individual councils to, in effect, set their own rates of educational progress, balanced educational planning for the country as a whole was made all the more difficult. In theory, of course, it lay within the power of the administration to delay new school development by disapproving estimates, but the closer Kenya came to self-government the greater was the political risk in doing so.

The District Education Board had several advantages, however, as a mechanism for educational advance. The fact that a foreseeable amount, depending on the fiscal ability of the ADC, could be counted on each year from the central administration made local educational planning easier over a period of years. Since the board was advisory and its advice could be overridden by the administration, it was possible for it to remain largely free of political pressure from the councilors. The Minister made appointments to the board on the recommendation of the District or Provincial Education Officer, creating a strong likelihood that interested and qualified citizens would be among the membership. Since independence, the County Council education committees, being confined to elected councilors, have not necessarily had this type of member. The DEBs were aided, of course, for much of the pre-independence period by the absence of formally constituted political parties, so that the question of balanced party representation on the board did not arise.

Despite the appointive nature of the DEBs, they are looked back upon both by the present County Education Officers and by some County Councils as model bodies for the administration of primary education. From the viewpoint of the CEO, a return to them would remove him from his present anomalous position and would restore his full executive powers.[17] The councils and the council staffs see them as a method of removing education from politics and putting it into the hands of those most qualified to deal with it and, incidentally, removing a subject from council debate that takes up inordinate time and is frequently the cause of a good deal of bitterness. But it is clear that there can be no return directly to a District Education Board formula, if for no other reason than that it was an institution created by the colonial administration. Moreover, control over primary education is a jealously guarded local power today, and it is very doubtful if a majority of councilors would agree to a system that took effective powers over it away from the council, the more so if this meant an enlargement of the role of the Provincial Administration.

Much of the history of African primary education in the colonial period revolved about three major questions, which have been alluded to in previous pages. The administration's struggle to balance rising costs against an even more rapidly growing demand for education is a continuous theme throughout the Director of Education's reports and in the numerous commissions that considered the question over the period. A variety of solutions was offered, ranging from complete financial control at the center to full local responsibility for primary education. The impression is left that the central administration would gladly at times have washed its hands of the whole problem, and, indeed, the trend was constantly toward devolution of power downward.

But it was equally clear that the Local Native Councils, even with the assistance of relatively impartial District Education Boards, were incapable of assuming full control, even if this had been financially possible. As education expanded, the central administration felt increasingly uncomfortable about its lack of ability to give the desired level of supervision both to the content and to the financial administration of education. The lack of trained personnel forced continuing reliance on the missions, which, for different reasons, came to be resented by both central and local authorities.

Without the missions, education could not have been carried on, especially in the early years. Yet the Local Native Councils increasingly resented their presence, both because they represented a foreign influence and because they interposed themselves between the people and the administration in a field in which popular feeling ran high. The missions themselves complicated the situation by ambivalence of their own objectives; the desire to evangelize diluted their value as educators in the eyes of both the Africans and the administration.

The objectives of the colonial primary education system were never fully defined, largely because they were never agreed to by the three parties concerned or, for that matter, within the parties themselves. The European settlers saw education as a way of making the African population more useful within the framework of a developing and presumably permanent European community. The administration's position itself was unclear. In some degree it saw education as a means of improving the life of the African, but at the same time it could not fail to be influenced by the settlers' views that African education should be directed toward producing a useful labor force. Many Africans who sought education, on the other hand, saw in it, albeit dimly, a method of escaping from the career restraints imposed by the administration and from the Christian ethic the missions sought to impose. To attain its objectives, each party groped for a measure of control over the system that would be compatible with its capabilities and its aims. But the search was defeated at every turn by the hard and inescapable facts of interdependence; each needed the other if the job of education was to be carried out at all.

Independent Kenya could not escape the colonial heritage in education any more than it could in any other field. Today, the psychology born of decades of jockeying for positions of power conditions the relationship between central government and local authorities in education. Still unable to sustain the cost of education, the local authorities look to the center for substantial help, but always with the lurking suspicion that acceptance of financial aid means the loss of control over an important segment of local power. And, while the role of the missions has been substantially reduced, there continues to exist an abnormal sensitivity to the very presence of managed schools. In its turn, the central government has never been able to shed its continuing doubts about the wisdom of permitting local authorities to have a substantial voice in education. These doubts have been reinforced since independence by evidence of the incompetence of some local authorities and by the new emphasis on national integration and coordinated economic development, in which primary education plays such a vitally important role.

This, then, is the setting in which the next act in the history of primary education will be played out. The attempts since independence to seek fresh bases for the relations between the various levels of government dealing with primary education will be a continuing concern of both government and the public at large.

The Transition to Independence

At independence (December 12, 1963), the District Education Boards disappeared with the apparatus of colonial control. The Majimbo (Federal) Constitution placed responsibility for primary education (with the exception of a few named schools) in the hands of the regional governments as one of the "matters that are within exclusive Legislative competence of Regional Assemblies."[18] The regions had in fact administered primary and secondary education since the commencement of internal self-government on June 1, 1963. Some regional governments retained responsibility for financing former government schools and all commitments for which the DEBs had been responsible. Others, in the course of 1964, passed on control over education to local authorities. The administrative structure necessary to carry out the powers granted to the regions had barely begun to function, however, when the decision was made to revert to a unitary form of government under the Republican Constitution, which came into effect on December 12, 1964.

The intervening year was largely one of confusion, since the process of dismantling the central Ministry of Education took a substantial period of time, and files that had just been collected and forwarded to the regions had to be brought together again in Nairobi. The regions ceased to be responsible for primary education on December 11, 1964, and for a brief period considerable budgetary turmoil ensued. Those schools that had been handed over to local authorities by regional governments continued to be financed by those authorities. But, for the fifty-odd that had been retained by regional governments, some method of interim support had to be found until central government decisions on the responsibility for primary education could be made and enforced.

It was ultimately decided that the ministry, for the period January to April 1965, pay grants to schools that could not have been included in the 1965 estimates of the local authorities and, in return, the ministry would collect school fees for them directly.

The government's decision to hand over administration and financing of primary education to local authorities was made early in 1965, and, using powers granted under an amendment to the Education Act of 1951, the Minister issued the Education (Entrustment of Functions to Local Authorities) Order.[19] On this legal basis the new County and Municipal Councils functioned in the field of primary education through the instrumentality of their education committees, which became, in effect, the local education authorities.

During the transitional period, two fundamental changes took place in primary education. The abolition of racial segregation within the system brought about the adoption of a common curriculum, and bursaries were offered to permit Africans to attend the high-cost former European and Asian schools (particularly at the secondary school level).

A second and equally significant change was the consolidation of the primary course into seven years, instead of the former four-year primary and four-year intermediate courses. The total amount of instruction remained as before, however, with the condensation of the first two years of primary school into one. The result was a rapid increase in the number of those taking the Kenya Preliminary Examination (KPE) in 1964, more than doubling the total for 1963. While the Ministry of Education could justifiably take pride in the expansion of education, the burden of providing additional teachers and facilities during this short period proved more than some local authorities could bear.

II

The Primary Education System
Since Independence

The return of full executive power to the central government with the end of regionalism meant that the Ministry of Education regained a large part of its former authority. Operating under the Education Act of 1951, the Minister assumed powers over the primary school syllabus, the certification of teachers, and approval of staffing, establishments, and standards for primary school premises. But much to the disappointment of the ministry, the most important instrument of control, financial power, was withheld by a governmental decision to channel all grants to local authorities through the Ministry of Local Government. While the Ministry of Education retained its powers over secondary education and teacher training, the earlier expectation that direct grants to the local authorities by the ministry would be the basis for the development of primary education never became a reality.

The reasons for this particular decision were never entirely elucidated; probably, it was in part the function of a desire to recentralize as far as possible, in view of the less than satisfactory provision of funds by the former Regional Assemblies. No doubt, too, there is a good deal of truth to the comment that "payment of grants by the Ministry of Local Government to cover the respective services for which different ministries were concerned, in consultation with these Ministries, appeared tidier and more convenient than payments by each Ministry." In the upshot the Ministry of Education reluctantly agreed, but only at the cost of a rather complex set of administrative procedures.

Estimates of primary education costs were prepared for the Ministry by each County and Municipal Education Officer annually and forwarded to Nairobi. Here they were examined and sent on with comment to the Ministry of Local Government. They were then collated with the overall estimates of expenditure prepared by each County and Municipal Council, but the total estimate could not be approved by the Minister of Local Government until the agreement of the Ministry of Education was certified to him. Inevitably, this required lengthy discussion between subordinate officials of each ministry over every case, resulting in inordinate delay in approval and consequent complaints from the local authorities. Since central government grants to local authorities were not earmarked for specific expenditure, the Ministry of Education anticipated that its representative in each local area would maintain educational accounts and no charge could be made against estimated expenditure except with his express consent. As the system turned out, however, this understanding was more honored in the breach than in the fact, for a variety of reasons that will be examined later.

With the disappearance of communally based education, the Ministry of Education was reorganized into a functional pattern under which the Chief Education Officer became responsible, with a deputy, for the development of all aspects of primary education. The link between the ministry and the schools consisted of the Provincial Education Officers (PEOs), including one for Nairobi, and below them the County Education Officers and their assistants (AEOs).[1]

It should be noted, however, that, while the ministry became responsible for supervision of curriculum and teachers, the schools themselves were, and still are, to a large degree, built by the communities. The capital costs of school construction are borne by the parents under the direction of a school committee, which raises funds and oversees the building and maintenance. The location of the school is negotiated with the CEO, and building standards are met according to his ruling. While some schools were built by the former African District Councils and some by the County Councils, the majority are still the work of the school committee. Thus the parents relieve the government of much of the otherwise sizeable factor of capital expenditure on primary schools.

Roles of the PEO and CEO

The post of Provincial Education Officer is in some ways supererogatory today; he remains almost as a holdover from the colonial period. In theory, his function is that of general coordination of and supervision over the CEOs in their administrative tasks. In addition, his office organizes and maintains the register of those sitting for the KPE. He is also responsible for coordination on two other levels of education, the secondary schools and the teacher training colleges in his province. But, since he has no veto powers over the actions of the County Councils on primary education, he can do little but express disapproval in his communications to the ministry. One PEO pointed out that he considered the post largely as a post office, passing papers stamped "approved" up and down the ladder of command.

In the earlier period, when ultimate control lay with the Director of Education, the PEO as his representative was able to exercise direct functional powers over the Provincial and District Education Boards. Today, the autonomous position of the County Councils in education leaves him little substantive authority. He remains an employee of the central government, but his relations are almost entirely with the secondary school system directly under the ministry. In a debate on the 1968 Education Bill, one member of the National Assembly voiced a commonly heard complaint:

> Unlike the colonial times when provincial education officers used to visit schools, see headmasters of schools, check the curriculum personally, you never see provincial education officers visiting any schools. If you go to a board of governors meeting you will find that a provincial education officer only goes to the office where the meeting is being held and back to his office . . . There is very little communication between the PEO and the CEO . . . I think the Ministry knows this very well; that the powers of the PEO's are not well used. The PEO leaves the CEO to do things according to the Council's direction.[2]

There is considerable justification to the complaint that the PEO has lost direct contact with much of the lower level of education today. The ministry's reply to this accusation is that, while admitting its accuracy, little can be done about it while the councils exercise direct control over the school system and the financial aspects must be shared with the Ministry of Local Government.

If the PEO has been cast in an indirect role, that of the CEO is even more uncertain and uncomfortable. The CEO's position derives its present difficulties from the fact that he is expected to serve two masters and, as a result, serves neither satisfactorily. He is an employee of the central government, seconded to the County Council. While remaining on the payroll of government, he is responsible to the council for the operation of primary schools in the county. Presumably he must take orders from above, while his primary responsibility is to his own council.

In practice this means that the CEO suffers from continually divided loyalty, made all the more acute because his orders from above and below are not infrequently contradictory. If he is to expect promotion within the ministry's service he cannot afford to alienate those above; if he fails to comply with the council's wishes, however ill-advised, he acquires the reputation at best of being "difficult" and at worst of being incompetent. Moreover, whatever his personal inclination, he is a member of the local community, subject to all the political pressures this implies, and if he exercises professional judgment counter to the community's wishes, he is likely to encounter social ostracism.

The CEO's functions are varied and very complex. He is at one and the same time the supervisor and director of education, the inspector of schools, the collector of school fees for most counties, and the general adviser to the public on education. He is responsible, among other duties, for preparing education estimates for the council's committee and for the ministry, for the hiring of suitable teachers and for the administration of school supplies. Clearly, virtually any one of these might constitute a full-time post; the result of the combination is that none gets his undivided attention. Since finances are a continuing and ever-pressing problem, they take priority and school inspection suffers accordingly. Many schools receive inspection visits only once a year, the more remote ones never. This would perhaps not be a critical point were trained teachers available, but the substantial percentage of untrained teachers in many schools means that without an inspector's help the standards of teaching are often lamentably low.

By far the most time-consuming and difficult task of the CEO is the collection of school fees. Fees are usually collected three times a year, at the opening of each term. The parents are notified of the day of collection in advance and, in theory at least, they appear at the school to pay and are issued a receipt by the headmaster. The CEO and his assistant education officers, accompanied by local police officers, tour the schools, picking up money to be deposited at a local bank or council office. In practice the process is by no means as simple. Inevitably, many parents are unable to pay by the appointed day, receipt books are lost, transport is unavailable, or weather makes the visit impossible, especially in remote areas in the rainy season. This necessitates repeated collection days, resulting in shortages of funds to pay teachers, inaccurate accounting, and mounting frustration on everyone's part, for which the hapless CEO must take the blame.

Interviews with CEOs throughout the country reveal that fee collection is the most resented part of the work. The officer feels that because of it he cannot do the professional work for which he was hired, and that it entails so much irritation on the part of the headmasters, the parents, and the council that it undermines any basis of confidence that might be established between the officer and the community. In some cases, where schools have been forced to close down and teachers discharged through failure to collect fees, feeling has become particularly bitter.

The problem of fee collection becomes further exacerbated by the involvement of headmasters in the task. Headmasters resent the additional responsibility; they face the ever-present temptation to petty theft or the possibility of loss when they are required to collect from parents who are unable to be present on the appointed collection day, and they see it as an intrusion on their professional duties. Both the CEOs and the headmasters argue that the poor showing of their students in the KPE examination is in part attributable to the time taken up in fee collection.[3]

The peculiar dual role in which the CEO is cast puts a premium on his skills as a diplomat and tactician as much as on his professional abilities. He must be on good working terms with the senior council staff, his committee, and the council as a whole, as well as with his teachers and with concerned members of the public. CEOs appear to be about evenly divided on the question of whether or not it is advisable to have a local man in the job. Qualifications being generally equal (to be appointed to the position requires both teaching qualification and experience), the effectiveness of the CEO depends upon his personality. Many argue that to be fully trusted one must come from the area, speak the local language, and be known personally or by family to the majority of councilors. In such a situation the CEO is freer to express opinions than an outsider would be, and he is more likely to be listened to because councilors tend to feel that he has the interests of the area genuinely at heart.

Almost the reverse set of arguments are advanced by those who are convinced that a CEO should never be posted to his home council. The very fact that he is known, and is familiar with the local situation, means that he is subject to a variety of pressures to which an outsider is more immune. The network of obligations created by the extended family system inevitably collides with his objective judgment. He is unable to offend those in authority on the council since he is related to them by other than professional ties, and in consequence he is under pressure to close his eyes to questionable ethical conduct on the part of the councilors. A local man is unwilling to make himself unpopular by his decisions because he must return to the community, even if he is subsequently posted elsewhere. A CEO from another area of the country may never become as fully familiar as a local man with the secrets and skeletons of local politics, but, by the same token, in his ignorance he is in a position to ride roughshod over sensibilities, which no local man can do.

There are, of course, basic truths on both sides. A local man may find it easier to persuade a council to make an unpalatable educational decision. And it is true that tribal affiliation does play a role in an officer's effectiveness at the local level; there are, for example, areas of Kenya in which a council would so distrust a man from another tribe that no real communication could ever be established. More than one Kikuyu CEO was vehement in his comment that he would refuse an appointment to a council of a Luo area; others expressed the view, however, that in the interest of an integrated society they would have no hesitation in accepting any posting, even if it meant more difficult personal relations. There is certainly some evidence that an officer posted to a part of the country with background similar to his own is likely to have greater understanding of the problems of local education. A man from West Pokot, for example, would be more effective in Kajiado County than on the coast because of his familiarity with the life of pastoral people.

A number of suggestions have been advanced to make the CEO's position more tenable. A majority of those interviewed would be opposed to making the CEO an employee of the council, for both professional and personal reasons. Professional advancement, it was argued, depended on connection to a central service that gave both posting mobility and continuing contact with advancements in education. Being part of a central service meant also a degree of job security that would not be possible under a council, where political pressures could result in abrupt termination of employment. Most CEOs favored a return to some type of education board, which would be in some degree autonomous from the council and to which the CEO would be answerable.

There was virtual unanimity on the question of fee collection—this should not be part of the CEO's duties. Some councils have already appreciated the fact that requiring the CEO to be a collector is a waste of his professional talents and experience and have turned to some other mechanism. Ministry officials have advanced the suggestion that fees be collected by the District Commissioner's staff as part of the graduated personal tax (GPT), but experience in the field would indicate that this is somewhat Utopian, since most farmers have difficulty producing the cash for minimum GPT payment; to ask for school fees at the same time would not be financially feasible and would produce severe political irritation by seeming to tie the unpopular GPT to education. One member of the legislature advanced an alternative in the course of debate:

> The collection of fees should be the responsibility of the chief's clerk. Parents ought to be told to pay their fees to the chief's clerk and the headmaster should be shown the receipt to indicate that such and such child has paid the fee.... It is no use having education officers being responsible for the collection of fees. At this stage they do no other work, do no supervision, they do no inspection, they do nothing.[4]

Councils, on the other hand, are not always anxious to have fee collection go into other hands. It might require employment of additional staff if it were left to them; they have, moreover, confidence in the accuracy of the CEOs' and headmasters' accounting because they can be counted on to be better educated than other council staff. If the District Commissioner does the job for the council, there is always the lurking suspicion that this is one more thin wedge into the council's powers. While most councils would be pleased to be rid of the problem of fees, they would not welcome any method that meant permanent removal of this source of council income.

Ideally, of course, the solution is to make the community responsible as a whole for the operation of the school system as part of the service provided by local government through the general tax structure, but this appears to be unlikely in the near future.[5]

The County Council's Role in Primary Education

The last link in the chain between the ministry and the school is the council's education committee. Under the Local Government Regulations, councils are empowered to appoint committees and to delegate to a committee, "any function exercisable by the local authority ... except the power of levying a rate ..."[6] All councils have created a committee to supervise primary education and, with the finance committee, it is usually the most active in the council. The education committee is responsible for the lion's share of every council's expenditure and, for this reason, if for no other, is frequently a source of controversy. Given the political importance of education, this committee reflects the political divisions within the council, as well as the interests of teachers and parents.

Particularly in rural areas, education has been the most popular plank in any councilor's election campaign; the promise of new or better schools is a sure way to garner votes, and candidates have made extravagant promises with little thought of the consequences. In the aftermath of Kenyan local elections, to an even greater degree than in elections elsewhere, casually made campaign promises for more education have been forcibly recalled to those elected. As a result there was, in the period immediately after the Jamhuri (Republic) Constitution, when the local authorities regained control over education, a marked tendency toward overexpansion of facilities with greater consideration for election promises than for cost. A combination of growing financial realism and reimposition of a measure of central control through estimate approval slowed down the pace somewhat, but still not rapidly enough to prevent many councils from reaching the point of bankruptcy. Despite the pleas of treasurers, many councils, responding both to real need and to political pressures, established new schools in remoter locations without considering recurrent costs—or if they did, made the automatic assumption that central government grants would make up the difference.

The composition of the education committees themselves compounded the problem for many councils, since they were, as were the councils as a whole for that matter, made up in large part of teachers. The tendency has been in rural areas in Kenya, as elsewhere in Africa, to elect teachers to representative bodies because of their educational attainments. Where both the finance and education committees had a majority of teachers as members, the two committees sat, in effect, as both judge and jury. They supported higher expenditure on education, more schools, and more costly trained teachers for political, personal, and professional reasons. In their efforts they were assured of public support, so that, under the circumstances, it was extremely difficult for the less well-educated farmers and traders who made up the rest of the membership to oppose them, even if they desired to do so.

The CEO, himself a former teacher, was as usual caught in the middle. He was aware of, and often objected to, overexpenditure, but at the same time his own interests were served by a greater number of schools and teachers under his supervision. In any case, he was scarcely in a position to question more education and so found it easier to give way to the council's inclinations, albeit against his better judgment. In those cases where the finance and the education committees disagreed on expenditure the CEO tended to become an involuntary arbitrator, inevitably at the expense of his own role.

Political considerations, often extraneous to the immediate issues, constantly plagued many councils. The CEOs interviewed insisted that politics constituted a major stumbling block to balanced educational development. In some councils in which the membership was evenly divided between parties, interparty rivalry reached the point where council action was delayed, if not entirely stultified. Endless and repetitious debate took place in committee that was comprehensible only if one understood local political personalities and issues. A committee report, hashed out in hours of meeting and representing a compromise reached only with great reluctance, could easily fail to find acceptance in full council meetings for no ascertainable reason other than the political interests of individual councilors.

Councilors were in many cases extremely sensitive to what they regarded as infringements on their sovereign authority by staff members. This was especially true in the education committee, where the teachers were prone to reject the advice of the CEO on the ground that they were as capable of knowing the right course of action as he was. Many of the older councilors resented being advised by "small boys," even when they were aware that the advice given was quite reasonable. They were unprepared to rubber-stamp a decision made by the CEO, although they might well arrive at the same point but only after a lengthy period of debate.

The problems created by the education committees are not, of course, unique to the councils in Kenya. Wherever development involves the generational gap and the rivalry between traditional and modern methods of decision-making, conflict of this nature is bound to occur. The senior councilors were right not only in their feeling that tradition lent authority to their decisions but also that they were, after all, the elected representatives of the people and expected to carry out their function to the best of their judgment. The trouble was that they were being called upon to make decisions in a modern realm for which their background had not fitted them, and in which they lacked the specific knowledge required for informed action.

But the fault was not all theirs. The younger CEOs were often intolerant of all but their peers and were unwilling to find the patience necessary to allow the committee to arrive at a decision by the traditionally discursive method. Moreover, their technical skills often blinded them to aspects of a question that, although political, was just as important to committee members as the substantive issue. Their "modern" approach was geared to thinking in terms of ministerial or legislative politics in Nairobi, and, because they saw education in terms of its function in the broader national context, they were unable to see its immediate place in the microcosm of county or locational politics. As one councilor succinctly put it, "It's all right for him [the CEO] to talk about closing schools in my location because not enough children go to them but he doesn't have to get elected next time."

The committee system is probably the most satisfactory method of insuring a measure of popular participation in educational decisions, although it is not necessarily the most efficient or, when it is a question of receiving tenders for school supplies, the most honest. An annual contract is arranged by the CEO and the clerk of the council with, at least theoretically, the lowest bidder as tenderer, but the system provides opportunity for graft at several points in the bidding process. The Ministry of Education has argued for some time that the system as it has operated since 1965 has failed to give adequate control from the center, and that it was not conducive to balanced development toward the goal of universal primary education. Since the ministry did not have ultimate control over estimates or grant expenditures, there was no way, it was claimed, by which long-range educational planning could be undertaken and budgetary restraints imposed on more progressive areas in order to enable backward areas, through assistance and encouragement, to catch up.

Local authorities were not, in the view of the ministry, adequately organized and staffed to undertake the supervision of primary education, nor was the CEO in a position to carry out the ministry's plans. It was also felt that councilors had to attain a higher level of education generally before the councils could be relied on to understand the delicate problems involved in operating a school system; the mistakes that had been made thus far provided, it was argued, ample proof of this contention.

Ministry officials agitated for a return to a local advisory group on education, on which the council would be represented but under which the CEO would hold executive powers as an employee of the ministry. Their efforts were crowned with at least partial success in 1967 and 1968 with the passage of the Teachers Service Commission Bill, establishing a single employer for all teachers at every level, and of the Education Act of 1968. But it remains to be seen whether the commission will solve either the personnel or the financial problems affecting primary education. More important, the question is raised whether the local authorities will permit, without strenuous political objection, the removal from their hands of power over a subject that has hitherto been one the councils have regarded as singularly their own.

The Teachers and the Teachers Service Commission

The superstructure of educational administration, important though it may be, can only be evaluated in terms of its success in dealing with the problems of those who are directly responsible for the education of children, the teachers themselves. The quality of the product of the educational system depends in considerable part on the skill of the teacher, but also on his psychological and material state and the degree of job satisfaction he derives from his work. It is not possible in this context to discuss the wide variety of questions involved in the content and design of teacher training in Kenya, nor its adequacy as far as the development now planned for the country is concerned. Our interest is rather in the place of the primary school teacher in the educational structure and in his relations both with his employer and within the community. More specific points regarding teachers' salaries as a factor in financing education will be raised in a later chapter.[7]

Kenya's 30,000-odd primary school teachers occupy a unique place in the country's social structure. They have been, in the rural areas particularly, in many ways a privileged group, at least in comparison with the peasant farmers, in terms both of income and status. As in other African countries, substantial numbers of those now in senior administrative posts, in the legislature, and in local government are former teachers, the products of the earlier mission schools. Because of their educational attainments, they carry some weight in a rural, largely illiterate community, and as a result are more likely to be chosen for positions of representative responsibility. In the past they were the leaders of modernization movements, and their opinions were listened to because of their ability to express the material goals of the villagers in writing. The spread of education and urbanization has reduced the teacher's role in the more developed parts of the country, but he remains virtually unchallenged in the remoter areas.

One consequence of the prominent role of teachers has been that they have, over a period of years, constituted a vocal and highly effective pressure group. Because of popular interest in education, the legislature and the government have found it very difficult to ignore the teachers' claims for better salaries and conditions of service and facilities. To this must be added the access of teachers to the legislators, in many cases themselves former teachers (who might very well have to return to the profession in the event of an electoral overturn). These factors have helped the Kenya National Union of Teachers (KNUT) create a powerful organization, one that has been successful both in bringing the complaints of teachers to the public attention and in promoting inquiries and legislation dealing with salaries and terms of employment. The union has been active in commenting on curriculum reform and in a number of aspects of teacher training as well. Its membership constitutes a majority of the primary school teachers, and is sufficiently strong so that a national teachers' strike, called in October 1965 over the issue of a single employer for all teachers in the country, as well as a variety of subsidiary issues, was successful; after four days government consented to appoint a commission to look into the problem of a single employer, which, following continued KNUT pressure, culminated in the passing of the Teachers Service Commission Act of 1966, which came into effect early in 1967.

The act climaxed a struggle that the teachers had been carrying on continuously since 1965, when control over primary education was returned to local authorities. Quite apart from the salary scales and grading of teachers, which formed another area of controversy with the central government, the teachers had been opposed from the outset to being employed by the County Councils. The basis of their opposition was twofold. They were opposed to the system by which councils could employ teachers on annual contract but lay them off at any time during the school year when it became clear that council funds were insufficient to pay all the teachers employed. Moreover, the councils had a strong tendency, when faced with financial restriction, to hire untrained teachers at a fraction of the salary that would be required, under government scales, for trained teachers. Because the councils were afraid of losing trained teachers, the untrained were the first to be dismissed when schools were closed, and this was the group that could least afford to be without employment.

As the financial situation became more critical for a number of councils, teacher layoffs and cases of failure to pay salaries continued to rise. Before the Teachers Service Commission Act came into operation in mid-1967, several hundred teachers were threatened. The union protested strongly to the ministry and talked of a national walkout; eventually emergency grants were found to tide the situation over, but the need for greater job security was evident both to the public and to the government.

The Teachers Service Commission Act was designed to create a central employer who would be responsible for the hiring and payment of primary teachers both in aided and unaided schools. Under the act the commission was empowered:

> to recruit and employ registered teachers, to assign teachers employed by the Commission for service in any public school, to promote or transfer any such teacher, to terminate the employment of any such teacher . . . and to delegate to any person or body . . . any of its powers under paragraph (a) of this section.[8]

For the purpose of maintaining full information on teachers, registration was undertaken of all those with qualifications; anyone refused registration could appeal to an Appeals Tribunal set up under the act. The commission was also empowered to remove a teacher from the registration rolls for sufficient cause, again with right of appeal. Under the act there was also established a Teachers Service Remuneration Committee, whose task it was to review teachers' salaries and recommend changes to the Minister of Education.

The crux of the new act, so far as the teachers' main complaint was concerned, is contained in Sections 16 and 17, "Financial Provisions." For teachers not assigned by the commission to local authorities, the Minister may make grants directly to the commission. But for the great majority of teachers who are employed by local authorities, the act failed to satisfy directly their basic claim.

Section 17, subsection (1) lays down that "where any teacher is assigned by the Commission for service in a school maintained or assisted by a local authority it shall be the duty of that local authority to make on behalf of the Commission prompt payment to that teacher of the remuneration due and payable to him by the Commission as his employer." The following subsection makes explicit that, "where in consequence of the failure of any local authority to discharge its duty under subsection (1) of this section, the Commission makes any payment of remuneration to a teacher that payment shall with interest . . . be due and payable by that local authority and shall be recoverable by the Commission and . . . it shall be the duty of the Minister . . . for Local Government to recover that debt on behalf of the Commission. . . ." Subsection (3) adds that, "for the purpose of ensuring that the Commission is at all times able to discharge its responsibilities as the employer of teachers assigned by the Commission for service in schools maintained or assisted by local authorities the Minister . . . for Local Government may . . . from time to time make advances to the Commission."

On the face of it, the provisions of these sections would appear to ensure the teachers of continuity of employment and payment by the commission, but, contrary to the expectations of the teachers, the local authorities remain the paying agents for the commission, and only in exceptional cases would the commission be the direct paymaster. In the course of planning the act, there had been discussed the transfer of an annual lump sum from local authority accounts to the commission, which would then make payments to teachers on its rolls. Two factors weighed against this, however: there was some objection by local authorities that this smacked too much of the return of central control over education; moreover, it was felt that the bureaucratic structure necessary to handle a large number of monthly payments from Nairobi would be extremely costly as well as unsatisfactory, given the uncertainty of postal communication in some areas.

The view of the teachers was that, while the act provided some assurance that they would ultimately be paid, they were still in the hands of local authorities as the commission's agents, and that when money ran out the commission might not have sufficient funds on hand to pay without lengthy negotiations with the Central Treasury. It would have been greatly preferable, they argued, if the central government had simply advanced all funds for teachers' salaries to the commission and collected from local authorities by withholding appropriate amounts of grant and GPT money.

The concept of the agency function of local authorities undoubtedly includes a number of pitfalls. While the commission is technically and legally the responsible employer, the money still comes from the local authority's treasury. In its education estimates, the authority may request a certain number of teachers to man its school system. It would be difficult for the commission to have sufficiently detailed knowledge of each local situation to be assured that the local authority really has sufficient prospective income to meet the salary requirements for the teachers requested. If there should be an overestimate or shortfall in its income, a local authority may well find itself (as many are at the moment) short of funds. At this point the commission becomes responsible for meeting salary demands. Indeed, there may well be a tendency on the part of the councils to overrequest numbers of teachers, secure in the knowledge that, if funds run out in midyear, they no longer risk public disapproval by having to release teachers and close schools. It is expected that, in cases where councils are unable to meet their obligations, the commission will engage in negotiations with the Central Treasury to make up the required difference in each individual case.

In theory, of course, the commission can control the assignment of teachers to limit educational expansion in any one local authority and to promote more balanced educational development by assignment of teachers to areas with fewer schools. Whether the commission will be prepared to take the political risks involved in such a step remains to be seen. Similarly, the Ministry of Local Government might well be able to make up monies advanced to the commission for delinquent local authorities by withholding from the annual bloc grant due to the councils. Here, again, however, political pressure may prevent such a step. Under these circumstances it is not unlikely that the councils will, in response to local pressures, continue to overexpand education, if there is every prospect they will ultimately be bailed out by the central government at no real cost to themselves.

Under the act, the commission is presumably free to assign teachers where they are needed, but in reality the teaching corps is by no means as flexible as the legislation appears to assume. Large numbers of the teachers interviewed in the course of my inquiry were adamant in their refusal to be reassigned to other than their home areas because a substantial part of their livelihood came from the *shambas* (farms) they owned nearby and that were operated by their wives, children, and members of the extended family. Many teachers interviewed pointed out that the demands made on them by family members for support and assistance with education meant that they had no prospect of being able to live on their salaries as teachers. So long as they are able to combine teaching and farming, they are able to survive reasonably well. If faced with being deprived of the farm income, however, their only alternative would be to resign from teaching. Undoubtedly a large number, particularly those who had been teaching long enough to be able to buy several acres of land (and were therefore the most experienced), would do so. The commission will not, of course, attempt wholesale transfers, but, where they become necessary, substantial inducement may have to be offered.

It is as yet too soon to estimate the cost, either in financial or political terms, of the commission. Its three initial members, appointed by the Minister of Education, were a former government personnel director, a former provincial commissioner, and a former teacher. They will enjoy a semiautonomous role, and will not be directly under government control. They will, however, be subject to severe pressures from the local authorities, from KNUT, and from the Central Treasury in carrying out their task. There always remains, in the background, the possibility that the commission might ultimately be used as an instrument for direct ministry control over primary education if the funds now used by local authorities for education under the bloc grant system were given directly to the commission. The ministry would probably give its wholehearted approval to such a step, as would KNUT, which has already publicly indicated that it does not find the present act satisfactory.

The teachers derive one secondary benefit from the act in that, as employees of the commission (legally a body corporate, separated from government) they are no longer regarded as servants of the local authorities and therefore subject, as government officers, to restrictions on their political activities. The question of teachers' participation in politics has been the cause of comment in the National Assembly, especially when the teacher concerned happened to be a member of the opposition party. Teachers have been accused of absenting themselves from classes to attend political meetings and of serving as party officials during teaching hours. While the ministry took the official position that the terms of service of teachers prevented them from undertaking other duties during classes, there was in fact comparatively little the ministry officers were prepared to do except in the most flagrant cases.[9]

There was always a somewhat delicate political question in the background. If the offender were a Kenya African National Union (KANU) local official (as he frequently was), the government bench, on the there-but-for-the-grace-of-God-go-I theory, was not prone to insist on disciplining the teacher. If he were an opposition supporter, the charge of suppressing the Kenya Peoples' Union (KPU) could always be raised. So long as teachers remained government officers, the same penalties for engaging in political activity could be applied to them as to any other civil servant, but now that they were the commission's employees, no direct retribution could be threatened. The teachers were firmly in favor of the new status, arguing that no distinction should be made between them and any other private citizens in pursuit of leisure-time activities.

The advent of the commission raised a number of subsidiary problems concerning discipline and control of teachers. Within a few months of the act's coming into force, complaints were already being made privately by CEOs and council members that teachers were becoming undisciplined, careless, and recalcitrant, claiming that the council could no longer dictate to them since it no longer employed them. In various parts of the country, at meetings held by the commission with CEOs and council staff members, questions were raised as to exactly what were the powers of the council as the commission's agent. Did they include discipline? Who approved transfers within a council's area? According to a Ministry of Local Government circular, CEOs were no longer to be involved in paying teachers; did this mean that the council would be required to find separate staff for the job? As agents, was the effective control of teachers in the hands of the County Council's education committee or in those of the CEO? These and many other questions of a like nature awaited resolution with both time and the experience of the commission.

The commission is also empowered to deal with teachers for unaided as well as aided schools. For the missions this will mean continued pressure for full Africanization of staff. Under the new regulations, missions cannot advertise for teachers locally without permission of the commission, and copies of indent forms for overseas teachers must be filed with it. No permanent appointments of expatriate mission teachers will be made, and the commission reserves the right to cancel a request for an expatriate teacher if a suitably qualified Kenyan can be recruited locally. All returning mission teachers will be appointed on temporary local terms and will be treated as any local teacher would be. The managers of the aided schools were not necessarily pleased by the loss of control over recruitment, but their continued operation depended on adhering to the commission's rulings.

The success of the machinery created under the act will depend in the final analysis on a growing supply of available teachers for the opening of prospective new schools and classes. As of March 1966, a total of 33,522 teachers were serving in Kenya's primary schools, of which 23,305 were trained and 10,217 untrained. More than 30.4 percent of the teaching force, therefore, was untrained; of this group nearly 8,000 had only the Kenya Preliminary Examination as qualification. As might be expected, there was a substantially higher percentage of untrained teachers in the rural areas, which, unlike the municipalities, could neither attract nor afford the higher-cost trained teachers. In Nairobi, for example, only 137 out of 1,609 teachers were untrained, while in Gusii County in Nyanza Province there were fewer trained than untrained (1,042 as compared with 1,178). As Table 2 indicates, the North Eastern Province (Wajir, Garissa, Mandera) shows a certain anomaly in this respect, having more trained than untrained teachers despite its remoteness from the centers of population. Here the few schools in the pastoral areas are largely boarding. The government has made every effort, through substantial induce-ment allowances, to provide high-quality education in areas that have been under dispute with Somalia, and trained teachers have been placed in the schools.

The high percentage of untrained teachers has been of concern to the ministry since independence, but even at present expansion rates, given the increased enrollments over past years, any hope of improvement seems very small. The 1966-70 Development Plan points out:

In 1964, 30% of all primary teachers were untrained and over 75% were primary school leavers. By 1965 the proportion of unqualified teachers had risen further to 35%. In order to reverse this trend and increase the number of trained teachers the plan for training colleges, when complete, will provide an output of 2,900 teachers per year compared with 2,250 in 1965. . . . In the interests of more efficient operation the number of training colleges will be reduced from 34 to 25 and the large majority will have a minimum of 250 students.[10]

The comparatively modest increase in teacher output evisaged in the plan would be barely enough to keep pace with the rising population of eligible children, even if the present structure of school fees were retained. If the

Table 2

Comprehensive Ranking of Counties (1966)

County	% of trained primary teachers	% of untrained primary teachers	(1966 est.) Expenditure on primary education per annum per pupil (in shillings)	Rank in terms of % of trained teachers	(1966 est.) Rank in terms of amount spent on teacher salaries
1. Kiambu	78.1	21.9	157	7	3
2. Murang'a	69.4	30.6	140	11	4
3. Nyeri	67.3	32.7	143	17	5
4. Nyandarua	66.9	33.1	157	19	18
5. Kirinyaga	69.0	31.0	141	13	14
6. Masaku	57.0	43.0	122	28	2
7. Kitui	58.4	41.6	145	26	15
8. Embu	67.2	32.8	126	18	16
9. Meru	65.5	34.4	125	21	7
10. Isiolo	47.6	52.4	164	30	31
11. Marsabit	52.8	47.2	164	29	26
12. Kilifi	69.3	30.7	170	12	19
13. Kwale	61.8	38.2	161	24	21
14. Taita-Taveta	83.4	16.6	145	3	20
15. Lamu	40.6	59.4	370	33	32
16. Tana River	72.3	27.7	360	10	25
17. Kisumu	67.5	32.5	138	16	6
18. S. Nyanza	63.5	36.5	152	23	10
19. Gusii	46.9	53.1	87	31	8
20. Kakamega	82.9	17.1	135	4	1
21. Bungoma	76.4	23.6	138	8	11
22. Busia	85.6	14.4	159	2	17
23. Kipsigis	57.1	42.9	138	27	12
24. Sirikwa	75.9	24.1	146	9	9
25. Cent. Rift	79.4	20.6	169	5	13
26. Olkejuado	68.1	31.9	192	14	24
27. Turkana	58.8	41.2	432	25	28
28. Samburu	41.3	58.7	301	32	22
29. Laikipia	63.7	36.3	204	30	22
30. Narok	68.1	31.9	199	15	23
31. Wajir	89.5	10.5	661	1	27
32. Garissa	66.6	33.4	485	20	29
33. Mandera	79.3	20.7	188	6	33

projected universal primary education became a reality, increased enrollment would push the proportion of untrained teachers to an even higher figure and would further emphasize the disparity in proportion of untrained to trained already existing in less advanced regions. The Education Commission, in its report made in 1965, looks forward to a staffing ratio of six trained to two untrained teachers per stream in each school.[11] While admitting that this was less than satisfactory, the commission added that even the substitution of one trained for an untrained teacher would take up most of the additional resources likely to become available.

Any major attempt to solve the problem of untrained teachers immediately runs up against the twin financial barriers of cost of training facilities and the recurrent cost of paying the higher salaries resulting. It has been estimated that even a crash program of summer upgrading, which would add 400 shillings to a teacher's pay, could cost between one half and one million pounds per year in additional salaries. It is, of course, possible to envisage doubling the intake of the training colleges by cutting the course to one year, but this would meet with resistance from the teachers already trained. And it would, in any case, add substantially to salary costs over the present costs for untrained teachers.

It is difficult to avoid the pessimistic conclusion that the mounting cost of teachers as well as capital equipment will not permit large-scale improvement in the quality of primary education over the next five years, even with present fee structure and normal increase in enrollment. Were universal primary education to become a reality, there would undoubtedly be a decline in quality because additional untrained teachers would have to be employed, or costs would rise substantially if more holders of higher qualifications (such as School Certificate) became available for training as teachers.[12]

One further aspect of educational planning will affect teacher quality and supply. The question of introducing Swahili as a national language throughout the primary school system has caused intense discussion since independence. The Ministry of Education issued a policy statement early in 1967 proposing that Swahili become a compulsory subject taught in primary and secondary schools and in teacher training colleges, and the Curriculum Development Center has been at work on the production of suitable textbooks. At a conference in April 1967, KNUT unanimously resolved in favor of Swahili as a national language and raised the objection that Swahili was allocated only three periods per week as opposed to ten periods for English which "undermined" the Swahili language.[13]

The controversy over the use of Swahili has many sides that cannot be gone into here. It has been claimed in some quarters that it is not a genuine national language for Kenya, that it is unlikely that suitable scientific vocabulary can be developed in it, and that in Uganda the decision was taken to promote English rather than Swahili because adoption of the latter would only seem to discourage the use of other vernaculars.

Whatever may be the merits of these claims, there is no doubt that strong pressures are being applied to bring about the adoption of Swahili. It is natural that, in view of the colonial past, there should be great interest in the development and use of a common indigenous language rather than continued use of the medium of communication of the colonial administration. Language has been one of the major tools of national integration over the whole period of modern nationalism, and East Africa is no exception. But the practical, as opposed to the emotional and political, issues arising from the introduction of Swahili as the medium of instruction at the primary level are formidable. Although most teachers have enough Swahili at the moment to engage in day-to-day conversation, this by no means implies that the majority is capable of teaching the language or using it as a medium of instruction. For those who are coastal speakers of Swahili, of course, the problem does not arise, but for the remainder, Swahili is a second (or third) language, and to bring these teachers to the standards necessary for proper teaching in the language would be both costly and time consuming. It would require extensive effort in summer crash programs or in-service courses during the year, which by no means all teachers would be happy to undertake. Textbook production costs are high, and a prerequisite even to the production of texts is agreement on what is to be the standard form of the language.

Desirable though a national African language may be, the cost of achieving its full use must be balanced off against the equally pressing demands for expansion of education on the present basis. The answer to the question cannot, however, be given in purely economic terms because it is essentially a political issue that will be resolved on the basis of criteria that may have little to do with monetary considerations.

The Primary School Population

The superstructure of primary education sketched in the preceding sections rests, of course, on the "product" of the educational system, the pupils themselves. Ultimately, success or failure of primary education depends on the relevance of the instruction offered and on the numbers of the eligible school population that can be accommodated within the limits set on the system by the financial resources available.

Since Kenyan independence, the availability of schooling has been an increasingly crucial political issue. At the national level, government policy has been from the outset to introduce universal primary education as rapidly as possible; the major stumbling block has been lack of both teachers and money.[14] In its campaign for the 1963 election, KANU rashly promised free universal primary education, a promise that has returned to haunt the government both in the legislature and in local political meetings. The issue is referred to repeatedly in legislative debates, and it is one of the favorite clubs used by the KPU opposition to beat the KANU majority. In one debate, for example, an opposition member returned to the attack in these terms:

> I would say that when KPU takes over the leadership of this country the first thing we will look into will be the conditions of our people, particularly those in the rural areas. We attach great importance to education . . . education is number one of our fundamental differences with the KANU government. . . . When we come into power we will . . . consider that we are committed to face primary education, this will be the first thing we do as soon as we take over.[15]

In the electoral contests for the County Councils, the promise of a new school is a standard electoral tactic; the result is often overexpenditure by a council to make good its members' campaign commitments.

It is difficult to secure exact figures on the percentage of the eligible primary school population for which schooling is now available. The figure used by the Education Commission of 60.7 percent in 1965 is probably too high; a more accurate overall figure would probably be 53 to 55 percent.[16] In the judgment of County Education Officers, the figure would be even somewhat lower. The problem revolves about an accurate estimate of the primary school age population; all that can be done is to project, on the accepted basis of a 3 percent population increase, the figures of the 1962 census, which are themselves open to question. Absolute figures for 1965 (1,010,889) and 1966 (1,043,416) for total primary school enrollment show an increase of 32,327 between the two years, or slightly over 3 percent.[17] As is to be expected, enrollments show wide variation throughout the country. In Central Province, for example, where development is at the highest level, it is probable that counties such as Kiambu, near Nairobi, have an enrollment rate of 90 percent or more of eligible children. Almost one quarter of the primary school pupils of the country are enrolled in this province alone. At the other extreme, the figure for North Eastern Province, with a total enrollment of only slightly over 2,000, may not be over 2 or 3 percent of those eligible.[18]

It does not necessarily follow, of course, that places are not available in schools for a number of those not now attending. Average enrollment per class differs almost as widely as do the total numbers. For the country as a whole it is thirty pupils per class, but it rises from eleven in Tana River County to thirty-seven in Gusii and is slightly higher in municipal schools. For the most part it would appear that rural schools could absorb at least a small number more per class; an effort is being made to consolidate uneconomic schools in outlying locations. School fees remain a real barrier, especially in those areas with a lower rate of economic activity. In the Moslem areas the percentage of girls attending school is considerably lower; the numbers fall off even more sharply from Standards V through VII. The pastoral areas will continue to have lower enrollments for some time to come, since boys are seen to be more useful herding livestock than spending time in school.

The usefulness of education is rapidly becoming more apparent to the pastoralists, however, as increasing numbers enter the money economy. Hence it is probable that government will need little urging to carry out the Education Commission's recommendation that "the main effort of government should be directed towards raising the level of enrollment in those areas in which the percentage falls seriously short of the national average."[19] It is much less certain that the added recommendation, "this can be done in part by manipulating school fees so as to provide financial inducements in the areas of low enrollment,"[20] will be found to be politically feasible. Indeed, the high cost to government of the boarding schools necessary for pastoral areas make it unlikely that there will be a general inclination to lower fees and thereby reduce the contribution to education, in these areas, of local government units.

Enrollment by standard indicates that there is a more or less normal dropout rate each year from Standards I through IV that is attributable to failures and to inability to continue fee payment. Despite the consolidation of the former primary and intermediate levels, there continues to be a substantial decline in enrollment after Standard IV; but it is significant of the changing attitude toward education in rural areas that the enrollment curve rises again in Standards VI and VII. This would appear to indicate that some students who are forced to drop out for financial reasons at the end of Standard IV (many parents are willing to pay for all of their younger children but, when fees rise, are unable to pay for older children beyond Standard IV) return to school after a period of two or three years, during which they have been able to save money for fees. The increased enrollment in Standards VI and VII is also to be accounted for in part by the consolidation of Standards VII and VIII and in substantial part by repeaters, seeking either to pass the KPE or to improve on a previous passing mark to gain entry to a government secondary school.

The number of repeaters in Standard VII (estimated by some to be as high as 25 percent in certain areas) highlights a basic problem of primary education that can only be raised here in the briefest form.[21] The numbers of those sitting for the primary school graduation examination, the KPE, rose along with enrollments. In 1959 there were 13,655, by 1964 the number had risen to 103,400, and by 1966 to 133,042. While only 48.5 percent of those who sat for the exam passed, it is clear that even then the production of KPE holders far exceeded the capacity of the secondary school system. Only between 10 and 12 percent of the successful candidates were able to secure places in government secondary schools. Others were placed in Harambee schools (harambee meaning roughly "pull together," used by cartmen as a cry), the community-built and -operated secondary schools that have mushroomed in central Kenya and for which the fees were three times those paid in government schools. Still a few more were able to enter teacher training colleges; but for the vast majority of those who at least achieved the Standard VII level, there was no possibility of further schooling.

The Development Plan, 1966-70, foresaw an increase of 53 percent in the number of places in Form I, the first year of secondary school. This was intentionally low in order to restrain the expansion of the secondary school pyramid to permit gradual absorption of graduates into the job market. However, the market failed to expand sufficiently rapidly to meet the supply, so that secondary school graduates have in many cases been forced to take jobs that before were filled by those who only had KPE. It became so clear that secondary schooling was a prerequisite to a career that pupils began to repeat Standard VII to attain marks high enough for secondary school entry, or were forced to go on to very expensive Harambee or even private schools (to which admission might often be gained without KPE). For those lacking the money for these alternatives, no other course was open but to seek work in the larger towns and cities, usually at the expense of a relative and very frequently without success, or to return to the parental farm, a prospect both psychologically and financially unwelcome.

The value of repeating the final year of primary school is clearly indicated by Dr. Brownstein's sample of representative counties, in which he discovered that of those investigated who had entered government secondary schools, 65.9 percent were repeaters; those in Harambee schools 83.1 percent, and those in private schools 39 percent. Not only does the number of repeaters swell the classes at Standard VII level, making teaching more difficult, but, as Dr. Brownstein points out, repeaters seeking higher marks reinforce their own numbers by providing unfair competition to those trying the examination for the first time, thereby causing further repeating within this group. In theory, government regulations forbid repeating except where there are vacant places, but headmasters who are concerned with fee income are more than inclined to close their eyes to infractions of the rules, and for political reasons the government is not prepared to insist on strict enforcement of school-leaving regulations.

The "school leavers" problem deserves much more attention than it has hitherto been given. Both government and private organizations are aware of its implications.[22] Even if, in order to prepare students for careers in modern agriculture, a significant restructuring of the primary school curriculum were undertaken, it would be effective only if the prospects were bright that an adequate living could be earned in agriculture. A member of the legislature has emphasized the point:

> We find that when boys finish their primary schools, after they have done KPE, they cannot do anything. They are hopeless people who cannot help themselves anywhere in our society. . . . We have KPE leavers roaming in the streets, going back to the villages and being a burden to the people at home. . . . It can be stopped by changing the curriculum in such a way that

the pupils are prepared for life. . . . An industry of some kind must be taught in these schools . . . it is important that we introduce not only agriculture in our schools much more than it is now—but also agricultural machinery management.[23]

While the primary school in Kenya today may prepare for the absolute minimum of contact with the modern world by teaching basic literacy, it by no means satisfies the needs of the pupils to gain a livelihood.

The increasing numbers of unabsorbed school leavers, coupled with the demand for universal primary education, may well lead, in the coming years, to an acute political crisis. Large groups of young people with basic skills of literacy feel that the government has failed to provide them with the means to earn a reasonable living and therefore has robbed them of the fruits of independence. The education they have received does not prepare them for white-collar jobs, nor does it make for an interest in work on the land or in problems of local development. It leads instead to frustration and discontent, the political relief for which is to seek a change in the system of government. In addition, dissatisfaction among the youth cannot but be reflected in the political behavior of the parents who have sacrificed to pay for the education of their children. Under these circumstances, education becomes a question of prime political importance at the point at which the young people are expected to enter the employment market. At the present time this point meets with the approval neither of the voters nor of the primary school graduate.

It is, of course, questionable whether another course of action might have been taken by any government since independence. The popular demand for expansion of educational facilities could not have been denied by any political group seeking power; both KANU and KPU are committed to universal primary education. The commitment remains, as does the demand, but the willingness to pay for it diminishes as parents find that KPE holders have increasing difficulty in finding employment; with the result that complaints by headmasters and education officers of failure to pay school fees are widespread. An effort is being made to introduce into the curriculum of the primary schools some further training in vocational agriculture and in practical mechanical subjects, but this can be pursued only within certain limits. The present seven-year curriculum has little if any room for a wider variety of subject matter. More could be added only at the expense of the essentials being taught now by teachers who already complain of overload.

The Education Commission rejected the idea of vocational training at the primary school level because the children in school were too young for it and because most occupations today needed more, not less, education.[24] The Hon. Laurence Sagini, then Minister of Education, shared the commission's stand, particularly with regard to agricultural training, when he said, "What I do not agree with is the idea that the primary course should be reformed to give children training in a particular kind of employment. *This is not the job of the primary school.*"[25] More significant, perhaps, is the fact that the teaching corps has a vested interest in the curriculum in its present form; the teachers are teaching what they were themselves taught. Any major revision introducing entirely new material such as is needed for progressive farming would require retooling of the teachers, a costly process that could only be carried on over their objections.

Experiments have been made of adding a further year to the primary school cycle, a year essentially devoted to the elementary teaching of those trades most needed in agricultural areas—a type of "village polytechnic"[26]—to promote education for self-employment. These centers have been established by local committees under the leadership of the Christian Council of Kenya in cooperation with the Ministry of Social Services. Here, again, however, the problem of staffing arises as well as that of additional costs. Since the students who attended the extra year would be overwhelmingly those who failed to secure a place in secondary schools, there would be some tendency for them to be regarded as "second-class citizens" condemned to rural life unless the extra year were part of a larger program that provided specific incentives for remaining on the land.

It is arguable that rural vocational education should not, in fact, be the province of the Ministry of Education but of those ministries more directly concerned with its ultimate use, the Ministries of Agriculture, Social Services, and of Planning. Cooperative efforts by those ministries, utilizing staff trained by them for the purpose, may produce programs more closely related to the immediate needs for skilled agricultural personnel than one administered by the Ministry of Education, whose concern is more directly for the formal educational process. It would be preferable that such a program be carried on outside the school system, in order to connect it more directly in the popular mind with the prospective economic advantages to be gained from specialized training in agriculture.

Absorbing the school leavers into productive activities that will be of ultimate assistance to national development will require long-term planning involving diversification in agriculture and substantial investment in sectors of the economy other than education. Indeed, this investment may require restricting the share of the national income devoted to primary education. To carry out such a program will demand an act of political courage on the part of government, but the courage required may be less than that necessary to meet the attacks of those whose education has partially prepared them for places in the modernizing sector of the economy that do not yet exist in sufficient numbers.

III

Financing Primary Education

The present system of financing primary education puts virtually the entire cost on the shoulders of the County and Municipal Councils. Of the estimated £ 8,295,279[1] to be spent on primary education in 1966, all but £ 1,595,562 was spent by County Councils serving essentially rural areas. Based on a primary school enrollment of 1,043,416 for the year, it was costing the Kenya taxpayer approximately £ 8 to provide a place in primary school; it can be expected that in coming years, with rising costs of salaries and equipment, this figure will rise. The Revised Development Plan calls for an expected expenditure of £ 20 per primary school place in capital costs, or, at present rates of population increase, £ 100 million by the year 2000. Even under the best of circumstances it is unrealistic to expect that national income will rise rapidly enough to permit such expenditure unless funds that might be applied to other high-priority development projects are to be diverted to education.

The County Councils are finding that educational expenditure is not only the highest single item in their budgets, but that even to maintain present expenditure levels many are having to exhaust reserves and are operating under deficits that are so large as to threaten councils with complete financial collapse. Municipalities, with their more efficient tax collection and limited areas, are not subject to the same pressures, but they too are reaching a point where primary education is becoming a killing burden.

The financial problem facing the County Councils derives essentially from a combination of rising costs and fixed income. The political pressures to open additional schools, combined with higher teachers' salaries and mounting costs of supplies, require expenditures that rise more rapidly than does income from school fees and the councils' general sources of revenue. The rates that can be charged for school fees, as well as the GPT, are fixed by the central government, as is the amount of the councils' grants from the Ministry of Local Government.[2] To the lack of flexible income sources must be added the inefficiency of the council's revenue collection services, which only serves to accentuate the financial imbalance.

Sources of Educational Income

School fees collected for each child in primary school are expected, in theory at least, to supply the bulk of the cost of the school system. Fees are established locally, within guidelines set by the ministry, and in 1966 ranged from 30 to 69 shillings for pupils in Standards I to III and 60 to 85 shillings for Standards IV through VII; each county's rate is set in accordance with its estimated needs but within relatively narrow limits. To this is added a flat rate of 15 shillings per pupil for school supplies. Counties have repeatedly requested raises in fees as deficits mount, but only in very exceptional cases has a raise been authorized, since the Minister will refuse to sanction rates that are much out of line with previous levels. Many councils have urged that the power to set fee levels be given to the councils themselves, but the ministry has thus far been adamant in retaining this power, in part out of fear that councils would set such high fees that parents would be discouraged from sending children to school, or conversely, that councils would reduce fees in the face of political pressure to a point where the central government would be forced to give greater direct subvention to education.

Whatever the rate set, there remains the problem of collection already mentioned. Estimates of fee income are prepared by the CEO on the basis of past enrollments and projected population increases, but at best they can only be educated guesses. Fee income can be affected during the year by factors over which the CEO has no control. Weather, crop failure, changes in agricultural prices, and a host of other variables, including the personality of the school's headmaster, can change income levels unexpectedly and substantially. In those areas where fees are collected by installment, collections for the initial period may measure up to expectations in cases where parents have saved to get a child into school, but later collections may fall off seriously when parents are short of cash.

The delicate question is then raised as to what should happen to the child who cannot pay: is he to be summarily ejected from school, and told to remain away until he can pay? Apart from humanitarian considerations, neither the headmasters nor the councilors are prepared to incur the wrath of parents by large-scale expulsions. As a result, a shortfall in fees does not necessarily mean a falling off in school attendance, although attendance does become smaller as the school year progresses and children are withdrawn for other reasons. Some county treasurers are much more insistent than others that children who fail to pay fees must be sent away, but this tends to lead to further complications.

Teachers who have been hired for the year may suddenly find themselves without jobs if their classes shrink as a result of a shortfall in fee estimates and the county is unable to pay salaries. In 1966 over two thousand teachers were dismissed for this reason.

Expansion of education has outpaced the income from school fees throughout the country so that the general funds of county treasuries have been called on to make up the difference. For the majority of counties in 1966, fees covered less than half the total expenditure; percentages of educational costs raised by fees range from 8 percent in Garissa County of North Eastern Province to 71 percent in Laikipia and Nyandarua counties. The question of substantial raises in school fees to require parents to share a greater part of the cost of education has been under discussion, but the impression gained from education officers is that in most areas of the country the upper limit is being reached in the ability of parents to pay. Collection is becoming more onerous, and many parents are unable to meet the higher costs of the upper standards for older children. A sharp rise in fees would cut back the school population so that the expected advantages of additional income might well be largely canceled out, unless it were accompanied by reduction in the number of teachers.

At present, each council is authorized to make remission of school fees in cases of proved indigence, and most councils remit from 5 to 10 percent of the total fees collectible. While remission of fees is highly desirable in cases where parents are clearly unable to pay, the practice has led to abuses, and there is widespread complaint that fees are remitted by the education committees for reasons of politics, not poverty. There is some evidence to support the complaint, but it would not appear to be prevalent enough to warrant withdrawal of powers of remission.

The GPT, the councils' largest source of general income, is determined, on every individual's income, on the basis of an assessment made by a collector (usually the District Commissioner or a council assessment committee) and at rates fixed by the central government.[3] For those in the wage sector the GPT is collected on a pay-as-you-earn formula, but for the vast majority of rural taxpayers tax is paid on estimated income from small *shambas*.

The GPT is, on the whole, an unsatisfactory form of tax because of its high incidence on the lower income groups in the society and because of abuses within the assessment system. Estimates of agricultural income are notoriously difficult to make, since they depend on variables such as weather, crop yield, and market prices, which are beyond the assessor's control. Inevitably political considerations enter into assessments made by council committees—a well-known member of the opposition frequently finds himself in a higher assessment bracket than his neighbor who supports the majority party.

Collection is both costly and time consuming; recalcitrant taxpayers (of whom there are as many in Kenya as in other parts of the world) must be sought out individually if they do not come forward to pay taxes voluntarily. Since large numbers of taxpayers pay only the minimum tax it is more costly and troublesome to bring them to court than the tax itself is worth. Taxpayers who maintain residence in their home localities but work in urban areas are expected to have part of their tax remitted to their home from their urban source of income, but rural councils can never be certain that all the tax due them has been returned from such large urban centers as Nairobi. As a result, the GPT collected by the cities is often retained at the expense of the rural areas.[4]

It has been suggested that school fees and the GPT be collected simultaneously to save administrative costs, but this idea has been discarded as undesirable because the small farmer has not enough cash on hand to pay both at the same time. Moreover, the central government has shown reluctance to connect, in the public mind, paying for educational services and payment of general tax, since this would tend to discourage school attendance.

It would be preferable, of course, if the burden of primary education could be a general charge on the community rather than one that falls directly on the parents of school-age children. The cost is already shared by the community in some degree, of course, since part of the general tax funds are used for education. However, the time is not yet ripe in Kenya for this larger shift. People are accustomed to school fees and are more inclined to pay for a service for which there is some visible return. The relationship between taxation and the level of government services is by no means clear as yet to the bulk of rural Kenyans; all too often, taxes are regarded as a form of compulsory support for an administration whose function is obscure and whose capacity for absorbing funds is endless. Not entirely successful efforts have been made to clarify this relationship by having Location Chiefs—who, the lowest level of the administration, come into most frequent direct contact with the people—collect school fees.

The third significant segment of local government revenue used for education is the bloc grant made annually by the Ministry of Local Government to councils. The grant, which has not hitherto been earmarked, becomes part of the general revenues of the councils to maintain local services. For many councils the government grant is entirely consumed at present to make up the education deficit, leaving other important services such as public health to depend on other available funds. Up to 1968, grants were made on a very rough computation of need balanced off by the funds the Treasury was prepared to make available in any one year. In 1968 a formula plan for grants was introduced, but since this will mean essentially a redistribution of approximately the same amount as before, only a few councils can count on increased revenue from this source; those whose expenditure on education is highest will not receive significant relief.

Expenditure on Education

Since 1964, virtually every County Council in Kenya has operated on a deficit, or, if it has been able to balance its budget, it has done so at the cost of depletion of reserves. Without exception, county officials attribute this overexpenditure to primary education. Twenty-one of thirty-three councils spent over half of their current income for 1966 on this budget line alone. Two spent over 80 percent and six over 70 percent. The group as a whole spent an average of 65 percent; the only exceptions, which lowered this average, were counties in the North Eastern Province, in whose nomadic areas school attendance is low.

As is to be expected, the highest percentage figures occur in the heavily populated counties of Western Province, Kakamega and Bungoma, followed by those of Nyanza and Central provinces. Of the £ 6,699,717 budgeted by counties in their education estimates, the three counties of Western Province spent almost £ 1 million pounds and the three of Nyanza Province over £ 1 million, as compared to £ 30,529 for the three in North Eastern Province and £ 325,044 for the five counties in Coast Province.

As these figures indicate, expenditure on education was not balanced either in terms of the resources available or in terms of national distribution. Central Province spent, to educate some 91 percent of their eligible children, over £ 1.5 million in five counties, and the Rift Valley Province's five counties spent almost £ 850,000 to provide schooling for between 45 and 50 percent of their children; in North Eastern Province over £ 30,000 was spent to educate slightly over 2 percent of the school-age group. In other words, almost a quarter-million children in Central Province were able to attend school at an average cost of 146 shillings, while two thousand children in the North Eastern Province cost an average of 300 shillings per child. The extra cost in this area is accounted for in part by the fact that most schools are of necessity boarding schools. As Table 3 indicates, the cost in Central Province is near the average for counties in the agricultural areas.

The major causes for inflated expenditure on education have been (1) the desire of County Councils to spread educational opportunities as widely as possible by establishing new schools in the remoter locations and (2) the increased use of trained teachers. New schools entail capital as well as recurrent costs, and, while many councils have been able to afford the initial cost of, say, £ 200 to establish a Standard I classroom and housing for a teacher for several areas in one year, little thought has been given in educational planning to the fact that each school will develop through six more standards, each requiring classroom space and teachers, plus housing for them. Only a half of the recurrent costs can be recovered from school fees, so that a school that may cost only slightly over £ 100 the first year may well cost nearly £ 1,500 yearly at the end

Table 3

Ranking of Counties by Educational Expenditure and Results

County	(1966 est.) Rank in terms of total am't spent on education	(1966 est.) Rank in terms of expenditure on primary education per pupil per annum	(1966 act.) Rank in terms of % passes of KPE	(1966 act.) Rank in terms of absolute passes of KPE	(1966 act.) Rank in terms of total candidates for KPE
1. Kiambu	1	17[2]	21	5	2
2. Murang'a	4	25	9	7	7
3. Nyeri	5	23	16	6	5
4. Nyandarua	18	17[2]	15	18	18
5. Kirinyaga	15	24	25	15	14
6. Masaku	3	32	18	4	3
7. Kitui	14	21[3]	22	16	15
8. Embu	17	30	5	14	16
9. Meru	7	31	1	8	8
10. Isiolo	30	13[1]	13	25	26
11. Marsabit	27	13[1]			
12. Kilifi	19	11	27	18	20
13. Kwale	21	15	26	22	22
14. Taita-Taveta	20	21[3]	29	21	19
15. Lamu	32	4	2	27	27
16. Tana River	25	5	28	26	25
17. Kisumu	6	26[4]	7	3	4
18. S. Nyanza	10	19	4	9	9
19. Gusii	9	33	6	2	6
20. Kakamega	2	26[4]	20	1	1
21. Bungoma	12	29	12	11	10
22. Busia	16	16	23	17	17
23. Kipsigis	11	26[4]	3	10	12
24. Sirikwa	8	20	11	12	11
25. Cent. Rift	13	12	10	13	13
26. Olkejuado	23	9	19	23	23
27. Turkana	26	3	30	31	31
28. Samburu	28	6			
29. Laikipia	22	7	8	20	21
30. Narok	24	8	17	24	24
31. Wajir	29	1	14	28	28
32. Garissa	31	2	31	30	29
33. Mandera	33	10	24	29	30

[1], [2], [3], [4] indicates equal figures.

of six years, even if account is taken of the fact that the community now pays the initial capital costs of construction.

Many councils have found that the actual cost is much higher if schools are double streamed and teachers' salaries rise. Placing schools in areas in which hitherto the nearest school was beyond walking distance for young children has encouraged higher enrollment in Standards I and II than was expected, so the overall impact of educational costs is constantly being more strongly felt. Murang'a County, for example, where financial problems are acute, saw the number of pupils entering school rise from 9,100 in 1965 to 11,431 in 1966 and 15,047 in 1967. If this enrollment level continues in the county, by 1972 there will be over 105,000 children in schools, as compared with 72,000 in 1967.

The fact that population estimates for the school-age group tend everywhere to be low has only added to the CEOs' problems of forecasting educational expansion. The ministry's ideal pupil-teacher ratio is 30 to 35, and CEOs, having been caught with too few teachers in the face of unexpected enrollments, tend to inflate the estimates of teacher needs to meet these contingencies. When the expected numbers do not always appear, or a shortfall in funds occurs, teachers are removed and schools closed.

A number of councils, faced with mounting deficits, and since 80 percent of the education budgets were going to teachers' salaries, hired untrained in place of trained teachers at considerably lower salaries. In many cases there was no alternative, since insufficient trained teachers were available and councils in the remoter areas could not attract trained staff. All but four counties had a majority of trained teachers in 1966, although several fell just above 50 percent (cf. Table 2, page 28). The counties of Western Province all averaged over 80 percent trained teachers; indeed, one county official commented, "Our only industry is teaching." The only other counties to reach this average were Wajir (where the few teachers in the schools were recruited with special allowances) and Taita-Taveta in Coast Province (but with 423 teachers as compared to 4,118 in the three counties of Western Province). But even employing untrained teachers did not justify the costs involved in retaining some schools. In Kisumu County, for example, 61 out of 416 schools had fewer than 20 pupils per teacher and an additional 204 schools had between 20 and 30 per teacher. The overall average enrollment in South Nyanza County schools was 20 per class, yet the council was in virtual bankruptcy through overexpenditure on education. Closing schools already established is both politically and educationally dangerous, but, unless central government is prepared to subsidize primary education in those counties whose inability to pay for the present schools has been clearly demonstrated, there would seem to be little alternative.

The relationship between expenditure on teacher training and success in bringing larger numbers of the primary school-age population to an agreed standard of education would appear to be questionable on a statistical basis. If an objective criterion, passing the KPE, were to be accepted as a test, it would appear that counties with a higher number of trained teachers do not necessarily achieve better results (Table 3). In 1966, Kakamega County, with 82.9 percent trained teachers, ranked twentieth among the counties in percentage passes of those sitting for the KPE, although it was first in total numbers of passes and in those sitting for the examination. Busia, with 85.6 percent trained teachers, succeeded in ranking twenty-third among the counties, although it was seventeenth in total number of passes and candidates. Gusii County, with only 46.9 percent trained teachers, ranked sixth in percentage of passes and second only to Kakamega in number of absolute passes. Kipsigis, with 57.1 percent trained teachers, ranked third in percentage of passes and tenth and twelfth in absolute passes and total candidates. Fuller calculations for all counties would appear to indicate that no statistically significant advantage can be established in favor of greater numbers of trained teachers in producing better results in graduations from primary school.

It is fully realized, of course, that variables inherent in any particular county school system may affect this conclusion and that the conclusion may not be valid for a single county over a period of time.

The simple correlation of trained or untrained teachers to percentage passes could be influenced by the quality of the examination papers produced by students in counties where more trained teachers had been in the school system over a longer period. Stiffer competition because of larger numbers of better students, or because of the greater rigor with which sets of higher-quality papers are marked, may mean fewer overall passes among those sitting the examination in these counties. An attempt to give greater balance in the number of passes between less well-developed and more highly developed counties might account for the higher number of passes in counties less able to hire trained teachers. Moreover, the criterion of passing the KPE may not reflect the quality of education being imparted; those who have been in school for seven years and who fail KPE are by no means "uneducated."

But quality in education is extremely difficult to measure objectively under any circumstances, and so long as failure to pass the KPE is regarded as a barrier to further educational progress into secondary school, higher expenditure on salaries for trained teachers would seem to be open to question. It might be suggested that the failure lies not with the teacher but with the form and standards of the KPE. It may well be, too, that too much is expected of the teacher under the conditions of the rural school operation, or that the curriculum of the teacher training colleges is defective in that it does not prepare the teacher to teach the materials required by the KPE.

While all of these factors may serve as partial explanation for the statistically lower record of passing under trained teachers, it would appear that the more likely explanation lies in the figures themselves, as they are applied to specific counties. If, under further analysis, individual counties with larger numbers of untrained teachers are abstracted from the national totals, a more positive picture of the results obtained through trained teachers is achieved. The very good passing results to be found in such counties as Gusii, Masaku, Kitui, and Meru, even with large numbers of untrained teachers, probably derives from the fact that these are more backward counties and the children attending schools are motivated to work harder to catch up with those who pass the KPE in the more developed counties. Both pupils and teachers are aware that they are at a disadvantage in comparison with the better training offered in the schools of neighboring counties.

The greater push engendered by this awareness may well cancel out the effects of poorer teaching by untrained teachers in many schools, and as a consequence statistically better results are obtained than in cases where trained teachers are working with less highly motivated pupils. A similar explanation is advanced by A. H. Somerset (in *Predicting Success in School Certificate*[5]) for anomalous results found in like areas in Uganda, and there would seem to be good grounds for assuming that the figures for certain counties in Kenya are affected by the same circumstances.

Assuming that one major objective of primary education is to produce students capable of going further up the educational ladder, it may be generally argued that the present structure is excessively costly in terms of possible results. Cross-section analysis based on 1966 levels of expenditure per county would indicate that for each additional thousand pounds spent on education as a whole, on an average seven more passes in the KPE would be produced; for each additional thousand pounds spent in teachers' salaries, slightly over eight additional passes would result.

One way, of course, to reduce the impact of rising costs would be to restrict entrance into primary schools by providing only a limited number of new places or by refusing to open new schools. Such a decision would, however, entail political consequences in today's Kenya that no county councilor would wish to face, nor, for that matter, would any member of the legislature.

The Future Costs of Education

Education today is costing more than the poorer counties can afford, and the more highly developed counties, which can afford to educate greater numbers, are presumably reaping a greater benefit, although even they are reaching a point where expansion will have to cease. The poorer counties also suffer in that places in secondary schools are allocated in proportion to the size of the primary system in each county, and this means that fewer KPE candidates go on from those counties with fewer primary schools. It is difficult to see, however, how any other system could be used without appearing to give a political preference to underdevelopment. As a Ministry of Education paper comments:

Any alternative would mean ceasing to use performance in KPE as the sole criterion for secondary selection, and would involve preferring less well qualified candidates from poorer provinces to some of those with better KPE results from more developed areas. This might in fact be a justifiable procedure, not only on political grounds but also from an educational standpoint. For if one assumes a roughly equal distribution of basic ability among children in Kenya, it might appear reasonable on academic grounds to accept lower performance standards from children from provinces less well endowed with primary educational facilities.[6]

It is very doubtful, however, whether the more highly developed counties, where the index of opportunity is higher, would permit any change that radically biased the secondary-school entrance requirement in favor of less well-endowed counties.

Even were this done, the poorer counties would continue to be at a disadvantage because of their inability to keep pace with the rising cost of teaching staff. The salaries of teachers in the primary and secondary schools have been the subject of repeated investigation since independence, of frequent discussion in the legislature, and of much publicity, often at the instigation of KNUT. Until 1968 the salary scales and terms of service were those established by the Pratt Commission in 1964. In 1965 salaries were again examined by a Ministry of Labour board of inquiry, but the report of the commission was tabled until the work of the Public Salaries Review Commission of 1967 was complete, since it dealt also with salaries of teachers. Government accepted the bulk of the review commission's recommendations, embodying its views in Sessional Paper No. 11 (1967).

The primary school teaching corps is divided for purposes of salary and grading into five categories:

1. P 4 (teachers who have received two years of training but have not passed the KPE).

2. P 3 (teachers with two years of training and the KPE).

3. P 2 (teachers with the Kenya Junior Secondary Examination [two years of secondary school and two years of training]).

4. P 1 (teachers who hold the School Certificate and have two years of training).

5. S 1 (teachers with the Higher School Certificate and two years of training).

Each category has a separate salary scale with a number of intermediate steps and internal efficiency bars. Table 4 indicates the number of teachers in each category; it will be seen that over 12 percent of trained teachers had not reached the KPE standard.

Both the Public Salaries Review Commission in 1967 and the Education Commission in 1965 shared the view that the employment of unqualified teachers should be reduced. The review commission commented: "We do not consider that the employment of teachers without a KPE should be granted to

Table 4

Distribution of Trained Teachers by Category

Category	Number	% of total number of trained teachers	% of total of all teachers
P 4	2,884	12.38	8.6
P 3	14,759	63.33	44.03
P 2	3,271	14.03	9.76
P 1	1,615	6.93	4.82
S 1	84 ⎱	3.33	2.31
Other	692 ⎰		
Total	23,305		
(Untrained)	(10,217)		
Total	33,522		

untrained teachers as we accept the view which has been put to us that persons without proper training should not seek to make a career in teaching."[7] The Education Commission takes the somewhat more realistic view that:

> We had hoped that a faster reduction in the participation of unqualified teachers would have proved possible. . . . The continued retention of unqualified teachers in substantial numbers . . . is the price which must be paid for adequate growth in a period of rapidly rising child population and we think that, on balance, the payment is justified.[8]

Perhaps a more sanguine view is that expressed in the Ministry's own paper, that ". . . it is by no means certain that Kenya can afford to pay the salary bill for a marked increase of better qualified teachers."[9] (Cf. Table 5.) The conclusion seems inescapable, however, that so long as the marked differential in salary between trained and untrained teachers continues to exist, and unless the Teachers Service Commission is prepared to make up the difference, there will be a temptation for hard-pressed local authorities to employ the untrained.

The general approach to teachers' salaries taken by both the Education Commission and the Public Salaries Review Commission reflects serious consideration by both bodies for the morale of teachers. The Education Commission felt that:

> The morale of the teaching force is influenced by a variety of circumstances, not all of them financial. . . . However the level of teachers salaries clearly occupies a prominent place in the list. . . . it is in our opinion necessary that the Government should ensure that the trend of teachers salaries does not dip below the trend of salaries generally and indeed shows, if possible, some improvement in comparison with salaries as a whole.[10]

Table 5

Cost of Raising Teacher Salaries

	Estimated cost (in pounds) 1967/68
P 4 teachers	85,000
P 3 teachers	370,000
P 2 teachers	80,000
P 1 teachers	50,000
S 1 teachers	10,000
AEOs	10,000
Untrained teachers	80,000
Responsibility allowances	93,000
	778,000

Source: Kenya, *Report of the Public Salaries Review Commission 1967,* p. 103.

The review commission three years later was more emphatic in stating that "we consider that rather large increases can be justified for the teaching service as there has been a tendency for teachers' salaries to lag behind those of persons with comparable qualifications in other fields of activity."[11] These views are shared by many members of the legislature, not only because they are themselves former teachers but because the teachers through KNUT have been able to operate as a successful pressure group. The debate on the government's Sessional Paper No. 11 on teachers' salaries gave opportunity for full discussion of the question. The leader of the parliamentary opposition, Mr. Odinga, stressed the necessity for equal treatment of teachers with other civil servants. Discussing the salary of the unqualified teacher, he commented:

This salary is very much lower than even the unskilled laborer's in the field at the present moment. It is very low and I do not subscribe to the idea of those people who say that simply because one is a teacher, he should actually be encouraged to receive a lower wage than any other servant of the state. . . . I hope that the Minister will consider that teachers' pay and terms of service which have been one of our biggest headaches and as such we should settle it once and for all and put them on proper terms and also try to be strict with them . . . they have a great service to do for the nation and as such, if they are well treated they should look after the future of our children.[12]

Several speakers returned to the theme of the lowest-paid teachers. One complained:

The pattern coming out [of proposed increases] is that the Commission and the Government have decided to award bigger increments as one gets higher up. I thought that the whole idea in this county is African Socialism and that this idea was to try to push the lower stratum of the service . . . so that we can narrow the gap between those who are paid very little, and those who are highly paid. I think here the Government and the Commission have missed the point.[13]

Another member emphasized clearly the place of the rural teacher:

I would like to raise one issue here . . . which I am sure the Commission did not see. This is the question of rural life versus urban life. The Minister may not have known that the teachers in the county represent the cream of rural life. . . . Apart from the county council staff the teachers are the largest stream in the reserve. . . . So far the country has been only concentrating on conditions in the towns and this is wrong because, after all, the towns respect [sic] a very small fraction of our Republic. . . . It is the "rural" Kenya that has the votes of this country . . .[14]

Another member went so far as to move a further review of P 4, P 3, P 2, and unqualified teachers' salaries after six months because, if teachers were still unhappy with the salaries, "I want to tell all those members who have been elected by rural voters that the blame is on them because they know what they are doing here . . . the people who are channeling the political force of this country . . . are the teachers."[15]

The same member vividly made a point which was echoed by many teachers interviewed when he continued:

In fact, life in the rural areas is at this time very difficult because these teachers, according to the African way of life, are surrounded by a lot of 'parasitic' people, a lot of people who want free things, people who want to be fed. Every lunch time, a teacher cannot take lunch with his family alone . . . so he can never swallow anything and that is why most of the teachers are so thin and we are ashamed to meet them, seeing they are teaching our children and they look very worried, very thin, very undignified . . .[16]

Throughout the debate members urged better salaries for teachers, even though they were aware that the recommendations of the Public Salaries Review Commission would involve additional expenditures of £ 778,000 on salaries for the first year alone. The bulk of this expenditure would come for P 3 teachers, as Table 6 indicates, since they would receive an additional £ 18 per year at once with raises to £ 21 and £ 24 in subsequent years. This the commission justified "by reference to the responsibilities which a P 3 teacher is required to accept immediately on appointment.[17] Increases in other grades were proportional, although it is significant that the expenditure on responsibility allowances for headmasters was to be greater by £ 13,000 than the total increase to untrained teachers.

Table 6

Scales of Teachers' Salaries

	Previous scales	New scales
	K £[a] per annum	K £ per annum
A) Unqualified Teachers		
Completed primary only	84	90
With KPE[b]	96	103–104
With KJSE[c]	108	117
With CSC[d]	240	252
With HSC,[e] one principal pass	300	330
With HSC, two principal passes	350	366
B) Qualified Teachers		
P 4	120–180	135–231
P 3	162–264	180–360
P 2	240–456	264–480
P 1	348–726	378–756
S 1	582–1110	684–1119
Graduate	804–1710	810–1710

Note: The government proposals for new scales follows closely the recommendations of the Public Salaries Review Commission of 1967. These were announced in Sessional Paper No. 11 of 1967, and are given in the above table.

In addition a responsibility allowance was granted to primary school headmasters of £ 6 per subordinate teaching post under their control, to a maximum of £ 240 per annum.

a Kenya pounds
b Kenya Preliminary Examination
c Kenya Junior Secondary Examination
d Cambridge School Certificate
e Higher School Certificate

The commission was conscious of the fact that the burden of the increases recommended would fall on the local authorities, but felt that their precarious financial position should not be a determinant in fixing salaries:

We are aware that the financial position of many authorities is far from sound and that they may find it difficult to pay increased salaries to teachers. We feel, however, that it is undesirable that the salaries for such an important section of the community as the primary school teachers should be dependent on the financial standing of local authorities. It seems to us that the correct approach to this matter is to fix teachers' salaries at what can be accepted as fair rates and, if it subsequently transpires that some local authorities are genuinely unable to pay those rates after taking all reasonable steps to put their finances in order, then we feel that there is an obligation on the Central Government to provide some measures of financial help so that the teachers can be paid adequate salaries.[18]

The same point was made more directly in the legislative debate: "My suggestion here is that if a county council finds it difficult to pay the teachers our

Government should take over those teachers straightaway until the respective county council is able to pay the salaries . . ."[19]

In its Sessional Paper No. 11 the government acknowledged the existence of the problem of local authority financing by quoting the paragraph from the commission's report, but added noncommittally, "the Government notes the views of the Commission but considers that adequate provision exists through the Teachers Service Commission Act 1966 to provide stability in the Teaching Service."[20] It is by no means clear precisely what the government's position is, however, in the case of those counties that fail to pay teachers assigned to them by the commission. As has been indicated in the previous section, the commission possesses no income to pay teachers, and it remains the responsibility of the counties to provide the necessary funds.

It is possible that the implication of the official comment is that the central government considers itself ultimately responsible for providing "stability," but at no point is there a clear statement of obligation on the government's part. The teachers are afforded better protection than heretofore by the presence of the commission, but only to the degree that the government is prepared to become the financial backer of its work. The likelihood that this will be required is made greater by the government's acceptance of recommendations for nearly £ 1 million of additional salary requirements in the face of near bankruptcy in several counties, which cannot be expected to pay their share of these new costs.

The Cost of Universal Primary Education

Public demand for universal primary education has been clearly expressed, and, as has been already pointed out, both the political parties and the government are committed to it. But the financial implications as well as the alternative methods for its introduction require much more study than has been given them thus far. As a first step, the popular notion must be dispelled of "free" education. Too many Kenyans are still under the impression that the arrival of universal primary education will be accompanied by the abolition of all school fees but without a corresponding rise in the general rate of GPT to compensate for the loss of fees. Since costs would be more evenly spread through the community, there would not, of course, be a rise in GPT corresponding to the school fees now charged, but there would nevertheless be sufficient addition so that the average taxpayer would certainly feel it.

A second point to be considered is that, in theory, to make education universal fees would be abolished. But this would in no sense "guarantee" universality because many parents in rural areas, at least those parents of this generation, would still not be prepared to send their children to school unless forced to. Moreover, many of the smaller counties could not, for some years, hope to prove sufficient facilities for all potential entrants, even with some central assistance. To make primary education genuinely universal would mean that some type of enforcement measure would be necessary for the pastoral areas, that special boarding facilities would have to be provided, and that the central government would have to provide the capital costs of schools (in some cases in the more settled areas as well).

Planning the introduction of universal primary education is, given the inaccuracy or unavailability of statistical information, a complex and often frustrating task. A number of methods might be used, each of which entails its own economic or political perils. Fees might be abolished simply by fiat throughout the system, which would, based on 1966 enrollments, entail an immediate loss of £ 3,343,669 in revenue. They might be abolished piecemeal, either year by year or by groups of years, starting at either end of the school cycle. They might also be reduced gradually in amount over a certain period, ending with total abolition at the end of, say, a seven-year period, or even more gradually, so that a period of ten or fourteen years might be envisaged. Alternatively, if the government sought to bring about greater balance within the school system fees might be abolished in whole or in part in certain areas that are less fully developed and retained for the rest of the country. This latter method would probably involve the greatest degree of political risk, since the less-developed areas would be receiving, at least temporarily, governmental preference; it might be less dangerous to subsidize such areas through additional grants or general tax reductions.

Immediate abolition of all fees would bring about, for most parts of the country, an immediate and occasionally overwhelming rise in entrants for Standard I, so that new facilities would be required in many counties simultaneously. The bulge would not, however, be confined to Standard I; an additional bulge would be created by the fact that a substantial number of those who had been forced to drop out at the higher standards because of inability to pay fees would now be able to return. Many of those seeking entry would probably be above the normal entry age for primary school, but it is highly unlikely that any government would find it politically possible to forbid entry to an overage group that had been hitherto unable to attend school through no fault of its own. In the normal course of events it would take a further six years to eliminate this first year of additional entrants, so the facilities would continue to be strained until the normal entry from the early-age group could be regained throughout the system.

If an even more pronounced bunching is to be avoided, great care would have to be taken in announcing the abolition of fees. If it were to be announced some time in advance, parents would naturally tend to withhold children for a year to await the disappearance of fees, thus adding substantially to those entering in the first year of abolition. As a result, costs of the extra classes needed would have to be added to the revenue losses in school fees for at least the first four years. This might be offset in some degree by making a very slow reduction in fees, so that it would not pay to withhold a child. Still another possibility would be complete abolition for Standards I-IV, with retention of reasonably high fees for Standards V-VII. This, however, would be in part defeating the whole idea of universality, and would undo much of the work just completed to erase the distinction between primary and intermediate schools. While it would undoubtedly represent very real savings to the local authorities, since the higher-cost teachers are normally to be found in the upper standards, where there would be fewer pupils, and while it would serve to hold down the numbers passing the KPE, such a solution would be politically unacceptable and educationally undesirable.

As an indication of what could happen with the complete abolition of fees at one time, the experience of Nigeria is highly illuminating. There is reason to suppose that at least some of the problems found there would be duplicated in the Kenya situation. The Western Region of Nigeria introduced free primary education on January 1, 1955. Local authorities were asked to collect education rates, but, since the majority were unable to do so, virtually the entire cost (94.6 percent) of primary education fell on the Regional Government.[21] In the Eastern Region, where free primary education was preceded by education rating, the experiment had to be given up even before the introduction of free primary education on January 1, 1957. Costs rose so abruptly that the regional government reintroduced fees again before the end of the year. These were slowly withdrawn, but even by 1962 fees of 100 shillings for Standard V and 160 shillings for Standards VI and VII were being charged. Rates of increase per year in number of pupils for the Eastern Region were 14 percent and for the Western Region 17.7 percent. In a number of areas of the Western Region, schools were completed but were forced to stand empty for a period because of a teacher shortage.

Under most alternative methods of abolishing fees, it can be expected that the net cost of primary education to the government over a seven-year period will at the minimum quadruple. Table 7, calculated on the basis of the five alternatives listed below, gives an indication of the effects of fee abolition:

Alternative 1: Abolition of all fees in 1967.

Alternative 2: Abolition of fees in two stages, a 50 percent reduction in 1967 and the remainder in 1968.

Alternative 3: A gradual reduction of fees from 1967 to 1973 beginning with Standard I in 1967, adding one standard each year.

Alternative 4: Gradual reduction but in reverse order, beginning with Standard VII in 1967. In both cases all fees would be abolished by 1973. Figures are based on an expected annual increase in enrollment of 5 percent.

Alternative 5: A similar reduction to that of Alternative 4, but allowing for a 10 percent annual increase in enrollment.

It will be evident from Table 7 that nearly three-quarters of the primary-school age group could be enrolled by 1970 without making any changes in the

Table 7

Cost and Enrollments with
Universal Primary Education Under
Various Alternatives

Alternative	Net cost to gov't. £ million		Total enrollment % of age group		Standard I enrollment % of age group	Year of attainment of full primary education
	1970	1973[a]	1970	1973	1970	
1	15.7	21.9[b]	92.1	105.0[c]	100	(1974)
2	15.4	21.6	90.3	103.0	100	(1974)
3	14.1	22.6	93.0	116.5	100	(1974)
4	11.9	19.1	75.3	86.9	74.9	(1979)
5	12.4	21.0	81.0	100.0	90.2	(1978)
If present fees remain unchanged	9.0	13.4	73.3	79.0	74.9	(1992)

[a] Assumed 3 percent increase in education costs per annum.
[b] If salaries and other costs rise more than 25 percent by 1973, estimate is too low.
[c] Over 100 percent = repeaters and backlog.

Source: Ministry of Education figures.

present scale of fees, but that full primary education would not be attained before 1992. To reach this point under Alternative 3 would mean an increased net cost of £ 17.5 million for primary education over the 1965 net cost of £ 5.1 million, but this is offset by an inevitable rise of £ 8.1 million, whether fees are abolished or not, as a result of rising prices and availability of trained teachers. The remaining £ 9.1 million is accounted for only in part (£ 3.3 million) by the additional teachers and facilities needed for the new pupils; £ 5 million represents the "loss" or contribution the government would have to make to replace fees now paid by parents.

While much of the problem of universal primary education revolves about cost, an added factor is the effect it would have on the quality of primary education as a whole. Unless the Development Plan expectations change, it is clear that the ratio of qualified to unqualified teachers will not improve by 1973. Even at a 5 percent annual enrollment increase under present conditions, 36 percent of the serving teachers will be untrained in 1973; if any of the alternative plans for fee abolition are used, by 1973 the proportion is likely to be over 50 percent. Accordingly, if government plans to proceed immediately with universal primary education, substantially more will have to be budgeted for teacher training facilities; in any case, due to a growing admixture of untrained teachers, the quality of education may well not improve.

Other indirect costs are concealed in the concept of universal primary education. Inevitably, if the number of primary school leavers is increased, the pressure for more places in secondary schools will grow and the problem of the utilization of school leavers will be magnified. While the abolition of fees would presumably permit diversion of the personal income now used for this purpose, its effect may well be an inflationary growth of the fees now paid in Harambee schools. Even now there is some raiding of P 1 teachers from the primary system by Harambee schools, which can afford to pay salaries above the government scale; such a tendency would, sooner or later, require either regulation of Harambee school salaries or the government's taking over the schools themselves. The capital cost of supplying the 1.5 million new school places required by 1973 (under Alternative 3) might well come to £ 30 million, based on the figure of £ 20 per place used in the Revised Development Plan.

For certain areas of the country the cost of universal primary education would be for substantially more than just the addition of classrooms and teachers. In the pastoral areas—which take in the entire North Eastern Province; Marsabit, Isiolo, and parts of Meru and Kitui counties of Eastern Province; Turkana, Samburu, and parts of Sirikwa, Laikipia, Narok, and Kajiado counties of Rift Valley Province; and, largely, Tana River and Lamu counties of Coast Province—boarding schools would have to be maintained. The Education Commission formulated figures on the cost of these schools for this area (cf. Table 8) and came to the conclusion that "boarding financed from public funds cannot provide the main solution to educational development owing to its

Table 8

*Cost of Boarding to Public Funds in the Pastoral Areas in
the Event of Universal Primary Education There*

Year	Children of primary school age	Cost of boarding if all boarding £
1965	168,500	3,370,000
1970	196,400	3,928,000
1975	232,000	4,640,000
1980	272,100	5,442,000

Note: The commission's figures assume all children would be boarding; changes in pastoral areas by 1980 (particularly in those bordering settled areas) make this assumption doubtful. A more accurate figure might be 50 percent boarding, which would make the cost by 1975 about £ 2,500,000.

Source: Kenya Education Commission, *Report*, para. 564.

exorbitant cost . . ."[22] The commission suggested the possibility of *manyatta* schools, that is, the assignment of a teacher to move with a nomadic group from one grazing area to another, but these teachers would have to be drawn from the nomadic groups and specially trained. The commission pointed out that the output of trained teachers from the nomadic areas was so small as to preclude any rapid expansion in numbers of schools of any type. Similar schools have been tried with considerable success by the former French administration in Mauritania for nomadic desert bands, but they have the built-in limitation that among nomadic groups there is little inclination to send children to school after the level of Standard IV.

The problem of schools in nomadic areas is fundamentally not one of providing costly boarding facilities but rather of providing economic incentives to demonstrate the value of education in the first instance. With the small enrollment of eligible children, greater numbers could be included in present facilities. Wider use could also be made of instruction by radio. But so long as the child retains his present worth as a herdboy in the economic scale of values, further provision for universal education will not be widely accepted.

The commission's conclusion on education for the nomads remains valid: "What is required is an economic plan which takes into account the creation of viable settled communities, upon which the educational and other services can be based."[23] A start has been made on this through enforced limitations on nomadic movement, which have come about as a result of disturbed conditions in the North Eastern Province over the past five years. The new settlements created have given the nomads a taste of sedentary life; what is missing, however, is the acquisition of new skills to provide a livelihood for those whom the military have forced into a new way of life.

One further point must be added to the indirect costs of universal primary education. The figures cited in preceding paragraphs concern facilities and teaching staff. The creation of new schools, particularly with relatively inexperienced teachers, will require additional administrative and inspectorial staff. It has already been pointed out that the system of inspection with the present number of schools is highly deficient; universal primary education would magnify this in marked degree unless concomitant plans were made to enlarge the supervisory staff. The cost of enlarged "administrative overhead" is extremely difficult to calculate in the absence of concrete plans for each county, but it is a factor that cannot be neglected in reckoning the overall cost.

The picture that emerges for universal primary education is not encouraging for the immediate future, unless the government in power is prepared to divert funds from other purposes to it. The present situation of the local authorities is such that many are already overspending on education, and to maintain the present levels will increasingly require central assistance. If it were possible to recoup at least as much (or more, through more efficient collection) in GPT to offset the loss in present school fees, there would only be enough to maintain the normal per annum increase in enrollment. A decision to abolish fees throughout the system immediately would probably necessitate a rise in GPT rates of such magnitude that it is doubtful if the government could afford to take the risk, even for such a popular issue as education. It is possible that a gradual abolition (such as that suggested under Alternative 3) could be sustained by an annual rise in the basic GPT rate, depending upon the general economic growth of the country. Perhaps the course of least resistance might be to extend the period of gradual reduction over fourteen years so that the additional costs might be partially absorbed by rising revenue generated by development, or perhaps sources of revenue other than GPT might be utilized for primary education.

Both political parties have publicly espoused universal primary education; according to its public statements KPU is prepared to embark on it as a matter of the utmost urgency, but its spokesmen appear to have given little thought to the cost of implementation. It remains, however, a powerful plank in the opposition party platform. A KPU speaker raised the question in the debate on the Education Act of 1968 in these terms:

> The Kenya Government had it in mind that free education would be brought into being before seven years after independence. . . . However now it appears that, according to our Development Plan, there is no future for this. It does not seem as if there will be free primary education some time unless the present government in power is changed.[24]

According to KPU's political philosophy, the financial demands of universal primary education would be met by large-scale redistribution of income within society.[25] KANU's hesitation is painted as temporizing while the benefits of development go to the ruling few of the government party. Even if KPU's plans were carried out, however, the estimated costs of universal primary education could not be met without seriously sacrificing some other aspect of development.

KANU's gradualist approach would appear to be much more in line with the economic capabilities of the country at the moment. Until some changes are made in the financial relationship between central and local government, or the operation of the primary education system is removed from the hands of local authorities, any move toward universal primary education will merely hasten the financial collapse of the County Councils. The government could, without undue risk, make a move in the direction of universal primary education by a token gesture of reducing fees in Standard VII as an earnest of future intentions. This would serve to blunt some of the criticism arising over the issue and would give time for more complete planning of a wider move. A first step in this direction can probably be found in the structural changes envisaged in the Education Act of 1968 and the regulations that have been laid down under the act.

IV

The Road Toward Change

The Education Act of 1968

Until 1968, the legal basis upon which the education system of Kenya rested was the Education Act of 1952. This act, although amended and modified in many respects by administrative regulation over the intervening fifteen years, had not undergone any thorough revision to take into account the changes in education brought about by independence, the short period of federalism, and the Republican Constitution. In the various constitutional documents and their amendments, education had been mentioned, but at no point had consolidated control over primary education been placed directly in the hands of the ministry concerned. The Ministry of Education had been for some time past unhappy with the piecemeal state of its powers, and particularly the divided control over financing that it shared with the Ministry of Local Government. Plans for a new education bill had been discussed since independence, but only in the spring of 1968 did these become concretized in an act that went part way, at least, to meet the ministry's requirements.

In introducing the debate on the act in the legislature, the newly appointed Minister of Education, Dr. Kiano, emphasized the need for the legislation because the 1952 act "was really racial in its background."[1] Gradual adaptation of the previous act in the years since 1952 had eliminated much of this, but it was nevertheless unsuitable for an independent Kenya. Moreover, the Education Act of 1952 had, as a result of its origins in the Beecher Report, paid substantial attention to the role of state-assisted schools—i.e., the mission schools. During the intervening period Kenyan education had become a public system, and legislation was needed to formalize the role of mission schools in this new context. The basic goal, then, was, in the Minister's words, "essentially to replace an old colonial Ordinance with a new Education Act. . . . What we are trying to do is provide the necessary machinery and to introduce some major reforms."[2] The 1968 act does provide new machinery, but it is open to question whether the "major reforms" contained in it attack the heart of the problems of primary education as they have developed today.

Basic to the operation of the act is the vesting of responsibility for educational progress in the hands of the Minister of Education. Clause 3 of the act provides that:

> It is the duty of the Minister to promote the education of the people of Kenya and the progressive development of institutions devoted to the promotion of such education and to secure the effective cooperation, under his general direction and control, of all public bodies concerned with education in carrying out the national policy for education.[3]

While this provision may not make any real change in the day-to-day operation of the system, in comparison with the former situation, the added element lies in the term "responsibility." Former education ordinances were couched in terms of "control" only, whereas the Education Act of 1968 places future educational planning in the hands of the Minister of Education.

The indefinite wording of the clause was clearly an attempt to make the Minister's powers as all-encompassing as possible so that educational planning and development becomes unambiguously a function of the central government. By implication, this constitutes a recentralizing of authority and a withdrawal of some areas of local concern. While local authorities may take the initiative in preparing new school plans, implementation is subject to the Minister's approval. This corrects the situation in which local authorities proceeded to open schools almost at will after independence, without thought of the financial consequences. The intent of this clause was made explicit by another Minister, the late Hon. Tom Mboya, in his comment on the bill:

> There is a need to have more Government say and control in the education of the people of the country. We can no longer continue with the system by which you have pockets of authority all over the country, deciding what and how to conduct education throughout the country. There must be established a definite area of Government control if we are going to implement our policies. . . . The very idea of building a nation means that Government must have the instruments by which to control education so that the products from the school reflect the society and the nation we want to build.[4]

In the exercise of his responsibilities, the act provides for the appointment of advisory councils by the Minister. These councils, of not less than ten or more than twenty, are appointed for three-year terms and are headed by an appointed chairman. Their duties are to advise on matters referred to them by the Minister.

In general, the legislature welcomed the idea, with assurances by the Minister that he would make full use of the councils; the members urged him, however, to make sure the councils were representative of the entire country. One member went so far as to appeal to the Minister to appoint members from KANU only because "the members of the party know exactly who can best put forward the views of the people." He was roundly rebuked by other members for this display of partisanship; they argued that appointment must be on the basis of merit and experience in education. However laudable this sentiment may be, the opportunity for political influence offered by the councils will be difficult for the Minister to resist, a fact of which the members were well aware.

The heart of the act, insofar as it relates to primary schools, comes in Clause 5, under which the Minister may "entrust any of his functions with respect to education to a local authority on such terms, conditions or restrictions as he may think fit." He may revoke, vary, or amend any entrustment made (5 [2]) and recover, in agreement with the Minister of Local Government, any expenditure incurred by the entrustment (5 [3], [4]). The Minister lost no time in proceeding under this clause. The Education (Entrustment of Functions to Local Authorities) Order of 1968 came into existence on April 4 to replace the similar order of 1965.[5] Under the order the thirty-three County Councils and seven Municipal Councils became the entrustees, as before, but their functions were more clearly defined and in general more limited. They are required to exercise the following functions: (1) the preparation of plans for opening or closing primary schools (the Minister must approve any plan of this type); (2) the preparation of estimates, receipt of grants (approved again by the Minister and by the Minister of Local Government) and receipt of school fees, as well as administration and dispersal of grants and fees; (3) the preparation of educational development plans for each council's area, to be approved by the Minister; (4) the administration of secondary school bursaries.

The net effect of these provisions is to place control over primary education expansion directly in the hands of the Minister and to withdraw from the hands of the councils their powers to establish schools where they see fit. It remains to be seen, however, whether the Minister, in view of the political pressures that can be exerted on him, will be able to exercise his powers of approval with sufficient strength to prevent unplanned expansion. The power conferred under this order is an important one and, if suitably used, could go far to restrain councils from increasing facilities beyond their financial capabilities. In some measure also the order provides the councils with protection from local pressure for more schools, since the council can always place the blame for failure to meet popular demand on refusal of ministerial approval.

The other functions of the council in primary education remain essentially as before, but it is noteworthy that the order provides that the Minister may now direct the council to procure school equipment from a specified source. This clause (2g) is intended to solve the perpetual problem of graft in the council's contracts for school supplies with local suppliers. A central tendering board will buy all supplies and the councils will then indent on the board for their needs. This will not only remove the temptation for extralegal payments but will reduce costs, since the board will be buying in greater bulk than any council could.

As previously, three "high-cost" primary schools are excepted from the order and remain under central control. These schools — the Hill School in Eldoret, Kitale Primary School, and Nyeri Primary School — were formerly European schools, and because of their better facilities and more highly trained staff, have been allowed to charge much higher fees than the ordinary public school. These schools have been the subject of heated controversy; the accusations leveled at them are that they are privileged oases for the children of ministers and for the wealthy members of the Indian community, and that by creating a class distinction they do not conform to the ideals of African Socialism.

Defending the continuation of these and similar secondary schools in Nairobi, the then Minister for Economic Planning, Mr. Mboya, admitted that they did create social distinction but claimed that the objective was to bring all schools up to their standards. They were being integrated by forced enrollment of an increasing percentage of Africans, and bursaries were to be provided for those who qualified to enter but who could not afford the cost. He dismissed the charge that they were schools for ministers' children as petty, saying, "I would quite seriously and strongly suggest that an African child is perhaps better off in the so-called African schools than in those other schools from the point of view of cultural and other development."[6] The case for the privileged schools would not appear to be a strong one; there is no necessary transfer of quality in education from them to other primary schools, and the argument that they set a standard to which other schools must be upgraded simply does not hold water, since there is little likelihood that any number of public schools will be able to have the physical plant of the excepted schools.

The new act makes an important change in the education committee of each council. As before, a local authority is required to appoint an education committee, whose reports it must consider before any action dealing with education may be taken. However, the act prescribes that the committee shall consist of ten councilors and five other members, three of whom must represent sponsors appointed by the local authority.[7] The committee is also expected to take into account the views of the education officer who must attend its meetings.

For some councils, where coopted outsiders have been sitting on the education committee, the act will make little change. But cooptation that was permissive before is now mandatory, although the councilors remain in the majority. It is of interest that in the debate on the bill, several speakers felt that the act did not go nearly far enough in giving autonomy to the education committee. Some advocated a separate education vote, independent of the rest of the council's estimates or a return to the former District Education Board system. One pointed out:

Each local authority should control the education vote, independent of any other vote. This means the education vote must be separate from other local votes in any district. When a school is opened we do not have to close the school as the local authority has failed to find the money. Previously when we were under the Colonial Government we had a district education board in each district and this board used to run for a full year ... no parent wishes to see his child suffer as a result of the local authority running out of money. ... In fact we might urge the local authority to give a grant to the board. The board would be responsible for the maintenance of education under the supervision of the district education officer.[8]

It is problematical whether the act as now written should be regarded as the thin edge of a wedge that will eventually take the power over primary education away from the County Councils. The Ministry of Education has pushed for separate primary school boards, and this is still its ultimate goal. The formalization of ministerial control over educational planning, and the prescription of the numbers and composition of the education committee, is a step forward toward divorcing the council from direct control, although the full council may still override the committee's decisions.

The next step would be to create an autonomous body to deal with education, a group that would administer its own funds received from grants by the central government and the councils. This would, in effect, recreate the District Education Board under a new label. But a number of hurdles would have to be overcome before this would be possible. So long as its powers are limited to approval of esimates and central funds continue to be given in the form of bloc grants by the Ministry of Local Government, the Ministry of Education will not have the power of the purse strings. Many councils insist that if primary education were removed from their budgets they would be able to avert financial ruin, but at the same time they would deeply resent the imposition of central power in this field. In any case, public opinion is far from being convinced that primary education should be administered from Nairobi, where it would be much more difficult to apply pressure than at the local level. Nevertheless, the explicit powers of the Teachers Service Commission are making heavy inroads on the councils' former position, opening the way for piecemeal erosion of local control.

The Education Act of 1968 provides that for each school under the local authorities there be created a school committee, appointed by the authority. The committee is to be composed of three persons nominated by the local authority (not necessarily councilors), three nominated by the parents, and three either nominated by the sponsor, if one has been appointed, or appointed by the local authority, and who must be "dedicated and experienced in the field of education."[9] The duties of the committee cover a broad field. In general it is required to advise the local authority on matters regarding the welfare of the pupils and the school, to oversee admissions and discipline, and, in the case of former mission schools, to maintain the religious tradition of the school.

School committees are not, of course, a completely new feature. They have existed informally and under formal legislation for some years. Their effectiveness has been in past, and will continue to be, dependent on local interest and on the initiative and personality of the headmaster. Many headmasters interviewed regarded the school committee as a group of ignorant and interfering busybodies and had as little as possible to do with it. But in other cases, where the headmaster had genuinely sought out the help of the committee, the community had responded by building self-help additions to the school and even staff housing where the local authority had been unable to find funds. The committee is intended to serve as a vehicle for maintaining parental interest in the schools and a sense of community responsibility, but any amount of detailed legislation will be of little help toward these ends if the basic concern is not there.

Before turning to the major issue of mission schools, some minor provisions of the act are worthy of comment. Clause 18 deals with provisions for inspection and the authority of inspectors to require headmasters to furnish details of the school's operation and, in particular, to submit to auditing of the school's accounts. The phraseology used regarding the inspector's right of entry is significant: "The Minister shall appoint officers with authority to enter and inspect any school *or any place at which it is reasonably suspected that a school is being conducted . . .*" (italics mine). This proviso covers the contingency of privately operated "cram" schools and the schools set up in remote locations that are meant to provide special tutoring for passing the KPE.

Part IX of the act empowers the Minister to make grants to schools for buildings, for the feeding of pupils, and for a variety of other purposes. While the powers entrusted under this section appear to be very wide, they will continue to be powers effectively exercised by the Minister only in respect to education other than at the primary level. The ministry's budget under the Development Estimates for 1967/68 makes no mention of direct aid to primary education, although £ 20,000 is allotted under the heading of "teacher training colleges."[10] It does not appear probable that the Treasury will be in a position to engage in further grants for primary education beyond those already contemplated in the grants deriving from the Ministry of Local Government, and the powers given in this part of the act will not apply to primary schools.

Mission Schools and the New Act

Among the provisions of the Education Act of 1968 that will have the most far-reaching effects, and that have caused greater controversy than any others, are those concerning the place of the primary schools operated by mission groups. The schools affected are those which were aided by the local authorities but not managed by them. Clause 7 requires that the managers (i.e., the missions) of such schools must transfer the management of the schools to the local authority within a period of six months, or, if they wish to continue the school under the previous management, they must continue it as an unaided school. However, where the school was managed by a religious group, and if the community signifies its desire to maintain the religious tradition of the school, the local authority must appoint the former manager as the school's "sponsor." If the former manager or any ten citizens object to the action of the local authority in appointing or failing to appoint the sponsor, appeal can be made to the Minister of Education. For sponsored schools the Teachers Service Commission will assign teachers, but in consultation with the sponsor insofar as practicable.

For those primary schools which the present managers choose to keep within the unaided category, the Minister may, on application, appoint a board of governors representing the managers and the community, and may suspend or force the resignation of boards that fail to perform their duties. Unaided schools are to be registered, and the Minister has the power to revoke the registration and close the school if suitable facilities and staff are not maintained. While these provisions may apply to certain mission schools, they are aimed equally at private entrepreneurs who seek to establish schools for their own profit and at schools established by community effort. The overall result is to make possible enforced ministry supervision over educational institutions of every level and type outside the public school system. The provisions provide the legal powers necessary to prevent the opening of schools that are not managed by suitably qualified individuals, that do not meet certain prescribed standards, and that are not "consistent with the needs of Kenya and the economical and efficient provision of public education."[11] Certificates indicating completion of a course of education can only be issued by the ministry as a protection for standards of training.

In common with other powers assigned under the act, the powers to regulate the opening and conduct of unaided schools depend for their efficacy on the Minister's willingness to overcome political opposition. Many privately operated schools undoubtedly exist more for personal gain than for the educational advancement of their students, but if the Minister were to exercise his powers to the fullest to close them down he might well encounter strong objections from both politically influential owners and from the public. Privately owned schools, however imperfect the instruction they offer may be, do serve the function of providing a form of "escape valve" for those who, because of the shortage of secondary school places, find no other opportunities for further education. To eliminate such schools would only serve to reinforce the opposition's claim that education beyond the primary school was to be the province of a selected élite within the society.

In introducing the act, the Minister was quite frank about the objective of the provisions for management of all aided schools by local authorities. After thanking the churches for their past contribution, he went on:

> If we make some changes here, it is not really a criticism of the churches as such, but rather to place the responsibility of managing our private schools in the hands of local authorities. Without actually kicking out the church . . . we are tricking the churches and telling them that, as far as the power to control primary education is concerned, we are taking that to the local authorities.[12]

He elucidated his point at a later stage in the debate:

> A question has been asked as to why we are doing this, as to why we are asking the local authorities to be the managers of those schools and taking away the managerial authority from the voluntary organizations. The point is this. Whether we like it or not we must accept the responsibility for getting our children educated and furthermore educated along the lines the national policy prefers. Therefore to place the responsibility for management on our own elected leaders, on our own local authorities and ultimately on the Ministry of Education and the Central Government to me is a big step forward. . . . It is no use saying that perhaps our people are not experienced enough. This is the language that was used during the colonial days when we were seeking our independence and we were told we were not ready for this, we were not ready for that. I say that the day has come for the people of Kenya to undertake the responsibility of running their primary education."[13]

Although the Minister assured the House repeatedly that the surrender of school management had been thoroughly discussed with the voluntary agencies during the drafting stages of the bill, some members appeared to be apprehensive that turning over power to the local authorities would mean that the schools would be completely divorced from their former religious affiliations. In reply it was emphasized that Clause 8 (3c) specified that religious instruction would be given, "in conformity with a syllabus prepared or approved by regulation after consultation with the sponsor," but this failed to allay their fears and they sought further assurance that the Minister would adhere to his definition of a sponsor as one who "occupies no position of power over the school but exercises the right to be consulted."[14]

Members' attitudes ranged from complete disapproval of the proposed action to full support. Mr. Muliro, in a strong statement, put the case for continuation of church management:

> What the Government must accept is that these district or county councils today, the majority of them are becoming inefficient because they are run by young politicians who themselves have no knowledge of what is going on in education, who themselves cannot create effective discipline or

management. Therefore to deprive Christian or church organizations of what they are doing today in order to hand over the work to the people who are less efficient, who are immature and incompetent . . . is a thing which the Hon. Members in this House . . . must consider very seriously . . . competition by various church organizations is what has caused tremendous progress . . . we find that because of [this] there have been more schools built.[15]

Fear of the intrusion of politics into education and religion was a theme to which several members returned. One stated the point succinctly: "Even politics has entered into our religion and politics and religion can really confuse a country."[16] Speakers from the Coast Province in particular were anxious to preserve the position of Islam in the educational structure. Secularizing the schools would, in their view, endanger the basis of religious teaching. They moved to amend the act to provide that a sponsor have the right to reject particular teachers assigned to the school by the Teachers Service Commission if they were not of the sponsor's religious persuasion. It was argued that:

The very principle that we are trying to safeguard here, that the feelings of the people of a given community who agree with given missionaries, that they should be given a certain kind of education in the area, will be completely eroded under the powers of the Teachers Service Commission by bringing Catholics there if that is an Anglican place or if it is a Catholic place by bringing a heathen there who has no religion.[17]

The Minister refused to budge on this point, however, on the ground that to give hiring rights to the sponsor would in effect nullify the legislation already passed, giving these powers to the Teachers Service Commission, but he reiterated that the sponsor would be consulted and that the commission would be expected to take the community's wishes into account. The amendment was defeated, as was a further amendment that would have permitted the sponsor to attend classes to satisfy himself that religious instruction was being properly given.

Those members who spoke in favor of the act included the opposition speakers, who agreed that the long-term goal was to put education in the hands of public authorities. They felt, however, that the time was inopportune because the government had not yet developed a long-range pattern and philosophy of education for national development. A leading opposition member argued:

It is all right to say that the local authorities should take over the schools but are the local authorities going to have adequate finances to run them? Are they also going to have the necessary moral discipline, the right pattern of discipline to inculcate into these schools? We hear in this House many times that many of these local authorities are being condemned, being banned, being dispersed and so on. Is this the position we want our education to be in? . . . I know people have different faiths . . . you have a pattern of belief, the pattern of values, the pattern of discipline that educates you and makes you a responsible person but if you are going to be educated in a sort of vacuum where there is no agreed value, no agreed policy, no agreed aim, what kind of education is going to come out of that place? . . . Many of our members were in fact educated in missionary schools because the Government could not afford the money. That is still going on now . . . if the Government cannot get adequate funds to run its affairs . . . and the missionaries have to finance the schools, have to give some discipline to the schools how can Government come in and say that they have to be the big bosses with regard to education?[18]

Other supporters of the act insisted that control by the local authorities would put an end to the duplication of facilities and internecine struggles resulting from the presence of several missionary bodies in one area that tended to create dissension within the community.

A point stressed repeatedly in the debate, and one that was emphasized in many interviews, was concern for consultation with the community before action was taken to deprive the missions of their rights as sponsors. The right of appeal by the former manager or by any ten citizens against a local authority's decision on sponsorship was both criticized and supported. The critics argued that it would be relatively simple for anyone to secure the support of ten citizens and consequently the Minister would be overrun with appeals. Moreover, many appeals would rest not on the merits of the case but on purely political grounds. While admitting that this was a possibility, the Minister defended the draft act on the ground that the citizens, particularly the parents, should have somewhere to go for their appeal, even if it meant more work for the Ministry:

I tell you the number of memoranda we get is fantastic. . . . We do get all these but the point is, is it right to shut the mouths of our people just because we are afraid that the Minister will be too busy? . . . If ten people who really have no case at all bring a memorandum we will spot immediately that this memorandum is not important. . . . If it was only one parent we could have thought he had been persuaded by a priest but when they begin to get about ten, then that is important, at least we begin to take attention of what they have in mind.[19]

The Minister sought further to reassure members that there was no intention of transferring ownership of the school buildings nor of the land to the local authority and that the property rights of any religious group would continue as before. To take into account the widespread demand for special attention to the parents of children in mission schools, the Minister proposed an amendment (8[4]), duly accepted by the House, which stated clearly: "In determining what are the wishes of the community served by a school, the local authority or the Minister shall give due weight to the wishes of the parents of the children of the school."

The lengthy and often very animated discussion centering around the continued role of the missions in education is significant for the future separation of church and state in Kenya. The missions took such a predominant place in primary education in the past that their role could not easily be set aside. Despite bitter early controversy over the missions, the people have become so accustomed to their function in education that the concept of an entirely public authority in control is looked upon by some at least with scepticism, by others (probably an older minority) with very real opposition. The result is a curiously ambivalent attitude: on the one hand a real desire to assert the sovereignty of popular control in the important field of education and on the other hand a lurking suspicion that government (particularly the local authorities) cannot be fully trusted to do as good a job as the missions have done. There is a sense of gratitude for the Christian spirit of selflessness displayed by many missionaries in bringing education to areas where no government agency was prepared to go even if the resources for it had been available. At the same time a certain sense of irritation is unavoidable, especially for those who believe that the missions were too often on the side of the administration in the anticolonial struggle.

The sentimental and religious tie to the missions struggles against the intellectual awareness that they represent an outside agency that, through influence on education, constitutes an infringement, however benign and indirect, on Kenyan national independence. The government's determination, embodied in the Education Act of 1968, to assert its power to embrace education at every level in a national development plan is generally applauded, but there is still a question of whether the state will be able to include in its oversight of primary education that element of Christian or other religious values which the missions, whatever their sect, did as a matter of normal training for the children placed in their care.

Mission involvement through sectarian interest in local politics has long been, and continues to be, resented. Throwing education entirely into the arena of local and national politics is regarded by many, however, as an equal, if not greater, threat to their real interest, as parents, in the best possible education for their children. Missionary doctrine and popular desire to retain the African tradition have clashed historically in Kenya, but in the background there always remained the colonial administration, upon which ultimate pressure could be applied for a decision. Where education is controlled by government there exists the possibility that it could become a political football to be tossed between competing ideologists — and the people of Kenya are aware that their children could be the losers in that game.

The attitude of the missions toward the action of government contains similarly ambivalent elements. Most missions have, of course, for some time faced the possibility of secularization of education, and many were privately, if not publicly, relieved to see it take place. The government was increasingly more able to shoulder the cost of education than were the private agencies. The missions themselves were being Africanized, so that the teaching function at the primary level was very largely in African hands; indeed, the missions could scarcely have hoped to recruit expatriate teachers in sufficient numbers, even if the opportunity to do so had existed.

The realization that their role in education was dwindling rapidly did not necessarily make the prospect of losing control any less palatable to the mission groups. Despite the Minister's solemn assurances that they were not only widely consulted but were in full agreement with the objectives of the act, it remains to be seen whether the missions will be content to be "sponsors" while their former schools come under the (to them) questionable management of the local authorities. Mission influence in the community, particularly in Catholic areas, is still of importance, and those who see their interests threatened are in a position to muster community pressure against the local education committee, whether the committee deserves it or not. There will always be fruitful ground, as the debates on the act made clear, for the contention that religious training is not being given its rightful place in the transferred schools; in the Islamic areas of the coast the question has already been raised.

There is little possibility that the combined pressure of the mission groups, if they were inclined to exert it, would be able to force a return to the system of voluntary agency control. But, given sufficient grounds, they would still be able to stir up community feeling to the point where the educational process could be seriously disrupted. Such grounds might derive from the fear that government control over education is only a first step toward other forms of state interference with religious rights. The key to the future posture of the missions is to be found partially in the attitude of the communities toward the transferred schools. If the local authorities give evidence of sound and, on the whole, apolitical management they will meet with community approval. But if they fail to take into account popular criticism, and if they seek to de-emphasize the religious aspect of the curriculum, they are almost sure to meet with community reaction, at least from the parents. Religion is still sufficiently meaningful to the generation educated largely in the mission schools that it cannot be ignored in the educational process, even though there may be general agreement with the claim of the state to manage the primary schools.

The government is aware that the transfer of additional schools to the local authorities will inevitably increase the financial burden of education, and to meet this in part a new formula has been devised that will serve to increase the bloc grants to the County Councils by a total of over £ 350,000 from 1967 to 1968. The effect of these increases will be felt more strongly in the less well-developed counties, as part of the government's plan to produce more balanced national development. The counties of North Eastern Province will probably not be able to expend fully the amounts for which they qualify under the new formula, so that the total increase is more potential than actual. Unfortunately, the application of the formula as it presently stands would mean little or no increase (or even a decrease) for the counties with the heaviest educational budgets. In these areas, if special dispensation is not made the councils will be unable to carry transferred schools and may have to turn to the sponsors for assistance. Alternatively the Teachers Service Commission may be forced to negotiate additional funds to pay teachers assigned to posts in the transferred schools.

The Education Act of 1968 marks the assumption by the government of Kenya of the complete control of primary education for the first time. Neither the political nor financial consequences of the act can yet be measured, for such consequences depend on the way in which the Minister exercises the broad new powers given him in the fields of educational planning and development. Firm leadership, freed insofar as possible of the taint of politics, could mean the tailoring of educational efforts to meet clearly defined development goals much more closely than has hitherto been possible. But all the changes envisaged by the act will have little purpose if the primary school graduates cannot be absorbed into gainful employment. More widespread education will be of small value if it serves only to produce greater numbers of young Kenyans for whom there is essentially little or no place in the society.

Conclusion

At the present stage of Kenya's development primary education absorbs a substantial share, not only of government income, but of the national income as a whole. Purely in terms of public and private expenditure, it constitutes one of the country's largest "industries" and it is the most pervasive of government services. Primary education affects over half the children of school age in the country and in the advanced areas a much larger percentage. Its multiplier effect can be indirectly felt, through contact with children attending school, in both the adult population and in those children who are not yet able to attend school. Nearly £ 9 million is expended annually on primary education by the local authorities alone, apart from the central government's outlays on teacher training colleges and ancillary educational services. Over half of the general grant to local authorities goes to primary education.

In terms of personal expenditure, for the bulk of rural families the largest cash outlay is in school fees.[1] The total of school fees is four-fifths of the amount collected through the GPT, and, for families at the minimum tax levels, five to ten times more may be expended on school fees than on direct taxes. Primary school teachers constitute the largest single occupational group (excluding farmers) in the country, almost twice the number employed in the next highest group, clerical workers. Their cost, even with the present numbers of relatively low-paid untrained teachers, constitutes the nation's largest salary bill. A teacher (trained but with no more than primary education) receives a higher wage than many skilled artisans, and a primary school employing trained teachers for the senior standards pays out in salaries an amount equal to that earned by a graduate agricultural specialist.

Primary education represents therefore a significant investment that both in capital and recurrent costs will continue to grow. To a certain extent, through the powers placed in the Minister's hands by the Education Act of 1968, the rate of growth can be controlled by the central government, although the Minister may be restrained in the full use of those powers by political pressures. Plans for educational expansion are posited on the government's estimates of the growth of national income and on the possibility that the political leaders will yield to the demand for universal primary education. It is clear, however, that the cost of any expansion involving even a modest increase of the burden now resting on local authorities will have to be met either from central government funds directly or by broadening the tax base of the local authorities. Raising school fees across the board is neither possible in some areas nor politically desirable in any area. Increasing GPT rates may be possible as agricultural income rises, but the government is as yet unwilling to associate increased educational facilities with general rates of taxation in the popular mind.

Even with minimal expansion, costs will rise as teachers' salaries go up and more high-cost teachers are brought into the system. But factors other than direct costs will affect the financial picture. The objectives of primary education as seen by the government will in part determine future costs. Insofar as the government regards primary education as an instrument for fostering national integration, costly restructuring of the curriculum and of the work of the teacher training colleges will be required. If a Swahili language program already under way is markedly increased, extensive in-service training will be necessary, as will additions to training college staff. Similarly, if more effective use of the primary school as a vehicle for preparing young people for agricultural vocations is desired, further changes in curricula, textbooks, and teacher training will be needed. An upgrading of the quality of primary education that involves any substantial reorientation of teachers now in service will involve new expenditures, as the New Primary Approach for English has already proved. As Francis Sutton has argued, "a building and some kind of teacher are minimum essentials and the first efforts of local authorities and the Ministry of Education may be expected to be directed to those essentials. But the hope for really effective primary education is likely to depend upon considerable inputs beyond the minimum essentials."[2]

The definition of "really effective" primary education is, of course, open to a multitude of interpretations. Much has been written about the necessity of "Africanizing" the curriculum. Few would argue that curricula modeled on those of developed countries, even with considerable adaptation, are most suitable for African schools. The built-in assumption in European-based curricula that primary school is the first step in a longer educational process does not hold true for 90 percent of Kenyan pupils. For them the extent of their education in a formal sense will be that required to pass the Kenya Preliminary Examination, but the question must be asked, preliminary to what? If the sole function of the primary school is to act as a feeder to secondary schools, and if the curriculum is based on this, the money spent on 90 percent of the pupils is likely to be a poor investment in terms of the immediate concerns of economic development. While it is true, as Philip Foster points out, that attempts to restructure the curriculum with the needs of Africa in mind were largely self-defeating because they would have effectively denied the African a place in the colonial sphere of economic activity, it does not follow that the spheres of economic activity should or will be as limited under independent governments.[3]

It is in fact becoming increasingly evident that the primary school system in Kenya, as elsewhere in Africa, is not fitting its product for any vocation, whether in the agricultural or the industrial sector. But by the same token there is a general absence of agreement on the methods by which it might be better adapted to produce young people who would be content to have their future life in a rural community. Where the young man was at an earlier period expected to enter an essentially European urban community in a semiskilled occupation, a European-oriented curriculum was at least partially satisfactory. If his future lies in farming, however, there clearly has to be some change. But any change in the material offered at the primary level must, if it is to be acceptable, be tied to an economic advantage to be gained through agricultural knowledge; as Fergus B. Wilson succinctly puts it, "it is absolutely useless trying to create among school children a love of the land and an interest in going into agriculture if agriculture – as in many developing countries – simply is not worth going into."[4] Argument has gone back and forth on the merits of introducing agricultural science at the primary level. This is not the place to pursue the viewpoints expressed. For our purposes it is sufficient to point out that, however desirable changes of this nature in the curriculum may be, they will be costly in additional teachers or retooling of the present ones. Apart from this, those teaching have a vested interest in the skills they now possess and are unlikely, without additional incentives, to wish to add new ones.

The primary educational system is, whether the government desires it or not, involved in the process of rural transformation. The question is whether the schools should be mere adjuncts to the process or whether there should be a conscious effort to direct education toward the fulfillment of certain more or less specific goals of rural change. It has been maintained that to create a curriculum that is aimed at the rural community would not be acceptable to urban schools and that, in any case, there is not enough time in a seven-year period to teach the basics of literacy as well as the elements of scientific agriculture. However, it would seem possible to relate the content of what is taught more closely to the life of the child outside the school.

In Nigeria, experiments have been tried in which the reading material given in schools is directly concerned with the proper cultivation of the major crop in an area – in this case, tobacco – in order to encourage the continued use after leaving school of the literacy skills learned there. A major objection to this lies in the cost, since this would imply tailoring curriculum content to various areas of the country rather than teaching a common syllabus. In Tanzania, the educational philosophy advanced as part of the self-reliance program of the government goes much further to make the school a center of community activity both for children and adults, in order to associate education with every aspect of daily life and to get away from the view that the school exists essentially outside the community. However, too exclusive an effort to relate the school to the community runs into the danger that rural education will parallel too closely the stage of economic development reached by the community itself rather than acting as an agent of progressive change.

It is perhaps inevitable and desirable that primary education should reflect the ideological stance of the governing group in the developing countries. The enunciation of a coherent educational philosophy aimed at national integration and development depends on agreement by the national community on common goals for the society. Steps have been taken in this direction in Tanzania, but Kenya has not yet begun to emphasize in the schools concrete applications of the general philosophy expressed in African Socialism. Bearing in mind that the changes made in the education system today will not leave their mark on the adult population until almost 1980, it would seem all the more urgent that the objectives of primary education be more fully explicated than they have been up to now.

The Control and Financing of Primary Education

Central to planning for expansion or major change in primary education are the powers of control and financing. In many ways these are two sides of the same coin; the attempts since independence to divide them three ways, among the Ministries of Education and Local Government and the County Councils, are at the root of many of the difficulties that have been experienced over the past three years. The pressures toward more centralized control are heavy, and the arguments for it, telling. There is considerable substance to the Ministry of Education's claim that no effective planning can be done without financial and administrative control over the primary education system. In this it is supported by the Ministry of Economic Planning's view that the goals of the national plan can be defeated by decentralized decision-making.

It is, moreover, difficult to deny the assertion that more efficient and effective collection and disbursement of funds could be made by the central government services than by the less well-trained staffs of County Councils. This assertion is, of course, posited on the assumption that ample professional auditing and inspection personnel is available at the center; this is, at the moment at least, far from being the case. Complete removal of primary education from the local authorities carries serious administrative objections. It would require substantial additions to the present central staff of the Ministry of Education, which probably would more than offset savings at the local level. It would in my view be excessively cumbersome (County Education Officers complain already of the difficulties of correspondence with the ministry) and would hinder any rapid or temporary adjustment to local needs. Certain aspects of central control, such as single tendering for school supplies, have real advantages, and these are being implemented now.

One of the arguments in favor of central control most frequently heard concerns the necessity for balanced national development. Since education is the largest item of expenditure in the councils' budgets, the more highly developed areas of the country, such as Central Province, have been able to afford greater local resources for education and have been able to provide school places for substantially higher percentages of the eligible children than the more backward areas. The central government has been seeking a formula whereby greater central subsidization could go to the less-developed areas to permit them to increase local services, including education, at a more rapid rate. Inevitably, any formula devised for this purpose runs into the political objection that the developed areas are being denied a fair share of the revenues that they earn for the central government. In Kenya this is particularly pointed, since many of the most progressive areas are those to which KANU owes a particular political debt for their participation in the struggle for independence.

Instead of restraining the educational advance of some areas while the remainder catch up, there would seem to be some merit in allowing the richer counties to progress within limits at their own rates, provided they are willing to pay for it. For the people of those counties who demand higher quality education and are willing to tax themselves locally for it, it would be possible to amend the Local Government Regulations to permit a degree of flexibility in local taxing powers. If, for example, a county were given permission to impose at its own option a specific tax earmarked for expansion of primary education, say, on petrol sold within the county, some specific advantages might accrue: (1) some of the pressure on the Central Treasury for increased grants might be relieved; (2) since the tax would be imposed by the local authority, it would be up to the councilors to decide whether they wished to take the political risk of imposing it; and (3) it would serve to emphasize for the public to a greater degree than at present the direct connection between the amount of tax paid and the quality and extent of the services rendered by local government.

While petrol may not necessarily be the most suitable taxable item, whatever is used as a basis should be a product that is an outgrowth of modern economic development. The wide use of vehicular transport, both private and public, derives from the growth of commerce and is evidence of accelerated development, so that a tax on some aspect of vehicular use would seem most appropriate. The type of tax used should be relatively easy to collect and should be demonstrably used for its declared purpose, education. Such a local tax would not interfere with adjustment of government grants to give a greater share to needier areas. It would in fact mean that the present limits imposed to wealthier counties could be maintained since there would be another, optional source of revenue available to them.

There are valid objections, both practical and theoretical, to hypothecated taxes. Moreover, the central government may well look with disfavor on the entry of local authorities into a tax field that has hitherto been reserved to it. But without some basis for differentiated tax rates, it is difficult to see how balanced development can be achieved in the face of internal political pressures. As the system stands at present, the more highly developed areas run the risk of being penalized for their development by having a ceiling imposed on central government help. Differentiation could be secured by varying the rate of GPT by county, but this would be less desirable than permissive additional taxation, since, in the setting of individual county rates by the center, it would open the door to accusations of political influence.

The direction taken by the Education Act of 1968 toward greater central control, particularly in regulating expansion of facilities, will help to alleviate the critical financial situation of the counties in meeting their obligations to primary education. But it constitutes no definitive solution to the problem, since the counties remain responsible for the larger part of the costs. Under present circumstances it is difficult if not impossible to reduce costs — indeed, the pressure is the other way. Contraction of the number of schools by consolidation is possible, and has been employed in a few areas, but it is highly undesirable politically. The number of children attending school could be reduced by a significant rise in school fees. Parents in most parts of the country are probably paying as much as they can reasonably be expected to afford in school fees, and any increase would work real hardship on those with school-age children, particularly in the rural areas. In any case, any action by the central government to enforce higher fees is open to the same political objection as cutting back on the number of schools.

The most satisfactory compromise between local control and financing and the possible advantages of greater centralization would be a return to a modified and updated form of the former District Education Boards. Placing primary education under a body distinct from the council but on which the council was represented would have several advantages: (1) it would remove education from direct political pressures in the Council and would permit greater use of interested citizens with specialized knowledge who are not council members; (2) it would enable the government to make direct, earmarked grants for education separate from the all-inclusive bloc grant now used and would obviate competition by various services for a larger share of the council's budget; (3) a separate body of this nature could become responsible through its appointed agents for the collection of school fees, thus reassuring the parents that the fees were being used for school purposes and not for the general expenses of the council; (4) if primary education were placed under a body whose sole concern was education, closer liaison could be established between the Ministry of

Education and the local education authority and with it greater financial supervision.

Such a "Primary Education Board" would establish its own estimates of income made up of school fees, government grants, and a specifically agreed-upon amount from the council's general funds based on expect GPT returns. The council treasurer would then simply meet the board's indent – say, quarterly – in a lump sum, a large part of which would go into teachers' salaries. Once the council had agreed on its total contribution for the year provision could be made much more simply in its budget than under the present piecemeal arrangements, where there exists always the danger that a substantial education deficit has to be made up three-fourths of the way through the year.

A device such as the Primary Education Board would not deny the elected representatives, the councilors, a voice in primary education at the county level because they would make up a large part of the board's membership. It would also not necessarily reduce the total amount now being devoted to education, although with more careful attention to planning this may be possible. But it would permit the council to pay greater attention to other local government services and would make council budgeting considerably easier. Hopefully, the board's membership would make it both more knowledgeable and more efficient than are the education committees now.

For reasons of practical administration but also, and more importantly, for its implication for the future of local government in Kenya, an alternative such as this would seem much preferable to direct ministerial control. Despite all the difficulties it entails, a voice in primary education is one of the most cherished powers inherent in county government. Without exception the councils interviewed were unwilling to give up local control over education entirely, though most would have been more than willing to surrender the financial burden. Their motives were perhaps not always as fully centered about the welfare of the children as they have had one believe, but fundamentally they regarded education to be of such importance that they were unwilling to entrust it to the hands either of educationists or of politicians. Their interest in primary education was essentially a personal one, and there was always a measure of distrust in the impersonal and often inflexible bureaucracy of Nairobi. They were prepared to admit that they had made mistakes in past educational planning, and that their zeal had frequently outrun their means. But the mistakes were their own, and they were by no means convinced that the ministry representatives, for all their training, might not have made more serious mistakes, which would have affected the interests of their children more profoundly.

Control at the local level over fields such as primary education, which are regarded by the people as crucial to their own interests, is one of the surest ways to preserve a vital structure of local government. At a period when the tendency is to concentrate power at the center, when the paternalism of national government too easily replaces that of the colonial administration, it becomes all the more important to retain a structure of local government with a genuine basis of local power of decision. Without a sound foundation of local administration that can withstand the shock of violent shifts in leadership at the top, and that can provide a continuity of government during periods of crisis, there is little prospect of long-range political stability. To deprive local government of its vitality and to make of it merely a badly coordinated arm of the central administration means only a further reduction in meaningful popular political participation. Primary education in Kenya is still regarded by the units of local government as a field they share as partners with the national administration. To take away their remaining powers in this important area would deprive the County Councils of much of their remaining importance in the public view.

The Future of Primary Education

The degree to which the next generation of Kenyans will have an opportunity for entry into the modernizing sector of the economy through elementary education depends on the decisions made by the generation now in power. Decisions regarding the form, extent, and quality of primary education are as much, if not more, political decisions as they are decisions in economics or educational theory. A development or a manpower plan can be effective only to the extent that those exercising political power are prepared to make and enforce the often unpopular decisions necessary to carry it out.

Primary education is simultaneously a lever for economic advance and for national integration. The basic tools to prepare the individual for a modernizing role can be imparted in the primary school curriculum, but they will be largely useless unless they remain meaningful in the life the young people will be leading in the immediate post-school years. Primary education is not only a prerequisite to further study, but, in a country such as Kenya where, for the immediate future at least, it constitutes the entire educational experience for well over three-quarters of the children who enter school, it becomes an end in itself. As such it must be integrated into a national philosophy of social and economic development much more closely than it has hitherto been in Kenya.

The government may regard the primary education system as an opportunity to create a consciousness of being a Kenyan, but unless there is a consensus on what it means to be a "good Kenyan" — a consensus that is embodied in the national social philosophy espoused by the political leadership — the schools cannot be expected to act as effective vehicles for inculcation of this philosophy and therefore for national integration. If the political process is regarded as a game in which the winner takes all, it will inevitably make integration of the diverse peoples constituting Kenya today all the more difficult, since little room will be left for divergent opinion within the national consensus. There always exists the danger that the schools will be expected to impart to the younger generation an interpretation of the political consensus that is essentially that of the ruling group and that is designed to create respect, not for national institutions of government, but rather for those who control the powers of government at any particular time.

Perhaps one way of combining the desire of the government to create national consciousness and the sense of possessing a common culture with the need to accommodate local diversity is through continued sharing of control over primary education. A common curriculum prescription combined with financial supervision gives to the central government the necessary powers of oversight while supervision of day-to-day operation of the schools, with an advisory hand in planning, permits local education committees to play the role for which they are best fitted, and allows parents some meaningful voice in the education of their children. Admittedly, the sharing of powers between the two groups demands flexibility on both sides, but without it local involvement and interest in the educational process may be greatly diminished. The sharing of powers may not be administratively as "tidy" as ministry officials might like, but less than total administrative efficiency may be one of the prices that must be paid for political socialization.

Greater efficiency might be obtained if the County Education Officer were given further training in the field of his relations with the local education authority. As things stand, he regards his job as too strictly that of administrative control, perhaps a hangover from the colonial period. If he were permitted some latitude for creating local initiative, and if he felt that he were being given greater responsibility − and credit − for the successful operation of the school system under his jurisdiction, he might be able to play a more constructive role than he does at the moment. But to do this, he must have more specific training for the job than CEOs have had to date.

Decisions involving the allocation of financial resources must represent a compromise by the central government among the conflicting claims of many areas of development. Inevitably political pressures play a role in these decisions, however fully the government may be committed to operating within an economic plan. It would be idle to pretend that a KANU government, publicly committed to universal primary education, could have severely restricted county expenditure on education in the immediate post-independence years without serious risk of alienating a good deal of its support in the rural areas. Even if the national leadership had attempted to make such a decision, it could scarcely have been carried over the protest of the party's backbenchers, whose political careers depended heavily on providing schools in their constituencies.

The path of least resistance, then, in this initial period, was to retain responsibility for primary education at the county level, over the better judgment of officers in the Ministry of Education. So long as the central government subsidized education through the bloc grant system, there was continuing evidence of KANU's interest in this all-important field, but at the same time the County Councils remained free to expand their school system within (or beyond) their financial capacities. When this expansion reached a point where many councils were faced with the alternatives of bankruptcy or closing down schools, the central government was able to come to the rescue with emergency assistance — and, incidentally, to garner whatever political credit could be gained from this action.

For those councils whose financial difficulties were too serious, the cost of this special central aid was dismissal and replacement of the elected representatives by an appointed commission of civil servants. If the councils concerned were made up of substantial numbers, or a majority, of members of the opposition party, their dismissal could always be cited as further evidence of the opposition's irresponsibility and inability to handle the business of national government. In some cases, then, retention of education powers at the local level paid off handsomely in political dividends for the center. But it should be added that even councils with a KANU majority were often forced into unwise expansion by internal pressures created by the personal rivalries or family interests of council members.

Maximizing the use of local resources for primary education served to free for other development uses central funds that might not otherwise have been available. In addition, the longer-range aim of the national government to associate tax payments directly with benefits in the form of government services in the popular mind was emphasized through local collection of school fees and GPT, most of which clearly went toward the costs of education. While parents have been prepared to pay for the educational opportunities of the primary schools, they will only continue to do so if it can be seen that there is genuine opportunity for the school leavers. And unless the government can take immediate steps to expand meaningful career avenues for the primary school graduates, the political credit that KANU has accumulated through the rapid expansion of education by the counties will be dissipated before the full effect of the investment in the infrastructure of modernization, both urban and rural, can be felt.

Table 9

Primary School Enrollment
By Provinces and Districts, 1965–67

	1965	1966	1967
Central Province			
Kiambu	66,409	75,315	80,651
Kirinyaga	25,010	25,103	26,727
Murang'a	69,889	72,421	76,179
Nyandarua	14,565	15,736	21,453
Nyeri	60,393	60,670	66,265
Thika Municipal	1,735	2,060	2,283
Total	238,001	251,305	273,558
Coast Province			
Kilifi	13,209	14,152	16,002
Kwale	7,686	7,956	8,332
Lamu	485	584	664
Mombasa Municipal	20,128	21,473	23,087
Taita-Taveta	14,392	13,911	15,312
Tana River	1,623	1,555	2,322
Total	57,523	59,631	65,719
Eastern Province			
Embu	21,805	20,706	24,179
Isiolo/Marsabit	722	1,821	2,321
Kitui	27,776	26,200	28,969
Masaku	95,039	92,053	104,095
Meru	53,765	63,682	67,123
Total	199,107	204,462	226,687
Nairobi	45,096	49,728	52,977
North Eastern Province			
Garissa	–	595	731
Mandera	912	986	584
Wajir	–	509	507
Total	912	2,090	1,822

84

Table 9 (Continued)

	1965	1966	1967
Nyanza Province			
Gusii	36,936	83,807	84,973
Kisumu County	76,315	61,142	61,520
Kisumu Municipal	4,076	4,436	4,644
South Nyanza	44,972	41,952	45,684
Total	162,299	191,337	196,821
Rift Valley Province			
Central Rift	34,262	27,202	34,070
Kipsigis	39,968	42,553	45,127
Laikipia	6,400	6,198	7,382
Nakuru Municipal	5,341	5,452	5,915
Narok County	2,554	4,516	4,935
Olkejuado	4,029	5,125	5,637
Samburu	2,386	1,427	1,736
Sirikwa	65,492	51,212	59,342
Turkana	840	1,215	1,181
Total	161,272	144,902	165,325
Western Province			
Bungoma	36,227	37,340	44,273
Busia	20,746	17,882	18,331
Kakamega	89,706	84,739	87,666
Total	146,679	139,961	150,270
Grand Total	1,010,889	1,043,416	1,133,179

Source: Kenya, *Statistical Abstract, 1967* (Nairobi: Statistics Division, Ministry of Economic Planning and Development, August 1967), p. 125 (Table 150).

Table 10

Pupils Enrolled

Primary Schools by Standard, 1966/67

Standard	1966			1967		
	Male	Female	Total	Male	Female	Total
I	112,056	81,853	193,909	131,421	97,348	228,769
II	95,840	70,270	166,110	105,939	77,695	183,634
III	90,358	62,561	152,919	96,442	69,198	165,640
IV	79,494	50,788	130,282	88,028	58,884	146,912
V	75,484	45,366	120,850	76,488	47,364	123,832
VI	87,844	44,870	132,714	88,300	48,548	136,848
VII	104,472	41,720	146,192	103,177	44,367	147,544
VIII	319	121	440			
Total	645,867	397,549	1,043,416	689,795	443,384	1,133,179

Source: Kenya, *Statistical Abstract, 1967* (Nairobi: Statistics Division, Ministry of Economic Planning and Development, August 1967), p. 124 (Table 148).

Table 11

Pupils Enrolled

By Type of School, 1958–67

	1958	1959	1960	1961	1962
Primary Schools	651,758	719,510	781,295	870,448	935,766
Secondary Schools	15,356	19,239	20,139	22,167	26,586
Teacher Training	3,545	3,867	4,089	3,897	3,927
Trade	1,114	1,228	1,712	2,094	1,443
Total	671,773	743,844	807,235	898,606	967,722

	1963	1964	1965	1966	1967
Primary Schools[a]	891,553	1,010,889	1,014,719	1,043,416	1,133,179
Secondary Schools[b]	30,120	35,921	47,976	63,193	77,681
Teacher Training	4,119	4,849	5,355	5,474	5,904
Trade	1,202	1,043	1,247	1,349	1,335
Total	926,994	1,056,532	1,065,467	1,113,432	1,218,099

[a] Including intermediate grades.

[b] Secondary technical schools are included from 1964.

Source: Kenya, *Statistical Abstract, 1967* (Nairobi: Statistics Division, Ministry of Economic Planning and Development, August 1967), p. 123 (Table 146).

Table 12

Number of Schools
By Type, 1958–67

	1958	1959	1960	1961	1962	1963	1964	1965	1966	1967
Primary[a]	4,691	4,876	5,206	5,725	6,198	6,058	5,150	5,078	5,699	5,959
Secondary[b]	81	98	91	105	142	151	222	336	400	453
Teacher Training	45	48	46	45	41	37	35	33	33	28[c]
Trade	5	5	18	21	9	7	8	8	8	7[d]
All Schools	4,822	5,027	5,361	5,896	6,390	6,253	5,415	5,455	6,140	6,447

[a] Including intermediate grades from 1963 onwards.
[b] Secondary technical schools are included from 1964.
[c] The drop in number of schools is due to amalgamation of several schools.
[d] The drop in this case is due to the exclusion of Kenya Polytechnic and Mombasa Technical Institute.

Source: Kenya, *Statistical Abstract, 1967* (Nairobi: Statistics Division, Ministry of Economic Planning and Development, August 1967), p. 123 (Table 145).

Table 13

Teachers in Service
By Type of School, 1958–67

	1958	1959	1960	1961	1962	1963	1964	1965	1966	1967
Primary Schools[a]	15,189	17,464	18,624	20,192	22,655	22,772	27,828	30,592	33,522	35,672
Secondary Schools[b]	969	919	1,188	1,316	1,392	1,530	2,000	2,494	3,004	3,586
Teacher Training	280	347	384	310	373	354	316	366	400	424
Trade	147	209	n.a.	233	241	267	n.a.	133	125	91
Total	16,585	18,939	20,196	22,051	24,661	24,923	30,144	33,585	37,051	39,773

a Including intermediate grades from 1963 onwards.
b Secondary technical schools are included from 1964.

Source: Kenya, *Statistical Abstract, 1967* (Nairobi: Statistics Division, Ministry of Economic Planning and Development, August 1967), p. 123 (Table 147).

Appendix

REPUBLIC OF KENYA

THE EDUCATION ACT 1968

No. 5 of 1968

Date of Assent: 6th February 1968

Date of Commencement: By Notice

**An Act of Parliament to provide for the regulation and
progressive development of education**

ENACTED by the Parliament of Kenya, as follows:—

Part I — Preliminary

1. This Act may be cited as the Education Act 1968 and shall come into operation on such date as the Minister may, by notice in the Gazette, appoint.

2. In this Act, except where the context otherwise requires—

"advisory council" means an advisory council established under section 4 of this Act;

"assisted school" means a school, other than a maintained school, which receives financial assistance from the Ministry or assistance from the Teachers Service Commission established by the Teachers Service Commission Act 1966;

"Board of Governors" means a Board of Governors established under Part III of this Act;

"curriculum" means all the subjects taught and all the activities provided at any school, and may include the time devoted to each subject and activity;

"the Institute" means the Kenya Institute of Education established by section 23 (1) of this Act;

"institution of higher education" means a university or a constituent college or institution of a university;

"local authority" means a county council or a municipal council constituted under the Local Government Regulations 1963;

"maintained school" means a school in respect of which the Ministry or a local authority accepts general financial responsibility for maintenance;

"manager" means any person or body of persons responsible for the management and conduct of a school and includes a Board;

"principal" includes headmaster;

"public funds" means the public funds of the Government or the public funds of a local authority;

"public school" means a school maintained or assisted out of public funds;

"pupil" means a person enrolled as a pupil or student in a school;

"qualified teacher" has the meaning for the time being assigned to it in the Teachers Service Commission (Qualifications for Registration) Regulations 1967;

"register" means the Register of Unaided Schools established under Part IV of this Act;

"school" means an institution in which not less than ten pupils receive regular instruction, or an assembly of not less than ten pupils for the purpose of receiving regular instruction, or an institution which provides regular instruction by correspondence, but does not include—

(a) any institution or assembly for which a Minister other than the Minister is responsible; or

(b) any institution or assembly in which the instruction is, in the opinion of the Minister, wholly or mainly of a religious character; or

(c) any institution for the purpose of training persons for admission to the ordained ministry of a religious order;

"school committee" means a school committee established under section 9 of this Act;

"syllabus" means a concise statement of the contents of a course of instruction in a subject or subjects;

"the Teachers Service Commission" means the Teachers Service Commission established by section 3 of the Teachers Service Commission Act 1966;

"unaided school" means a school which is not receiving grants out of public funds.

Part II — Promotion of Education

3. (1) It is the duty of the Minister to promote the education of the people of Kenya and the progressive development of institutions devoted to the promotion of such education, and to secure the effective co-operation, under his general

direction or control, of all public bodies concerned with education in carrying out the national policy for education.

(2) For the purposes of carrying out his duties under subsection (1) of this section, the Minister may from time to time formulate a development plan for education consistent with any national plan for economic and social development of Kenya.

4. (1) The Minister may, by order, establish an advisory council to advise him on any matter concerning education in Kenya or in some part of Kenya, and may establish different councils for different areas or for different aspects of education.

(2) An advisory council shall consist of not less than ten and not more than twenty persons, each appointed by the Minister, and the Minister shall appoint one of the members to be chairman.

(3) The First Schedule of this Act shall apply with respect to advisory councils.

5. (1) Subject to this Act and to any regulations made thereunder, the Minister may, by order, entrust any of his functions with respect to education to a local authority on such terms, conditions or restrictions as he may think fit.

(2) The Minister may, by order, revoke, suspend, vary or amend an entrustment made under subsection (1) of this section.

(3) Where an entrustment of a function to a local authority is revoked or suspended under subsection (2) of this section, the Minister may recover from the local authority the whole or any part of the expenditure incurred in the performance of the functions:

Provided that, where the estimates of expenditure to be incurred by the local authority in the performance of the function are subject to the approval of the Minister for the time being responsible for local government under Part XV of the Local Government Regulations 1963, such recovery shall be subject to the agreement of the Minister for the time being responsible for local government.

(4) Where functions have been entrusted to a local authority under this section the local authority shall appoint an education committee in accordance with regulation 91 of the Local Government Regulations 1963, and shall consider a report from such education committee before exercising any of the functions:

Provided that, notwithstanding that regulation, an education committee shall consist of ten councillors and five other members appointed by the Minister, and those five other members shall include not more than three persons to represent any sponsor or sponsors appointed by the local authority under section 8 (1) of the Act.

(5) The principal education officer of a local authority shall attend all meetings of an education committee appointed under subsection (4) of this section, and shall advise the local authority on all matters concerning education in the area of the local authority.

Part III — Management of Schools

General

6. Subject to section 7 of this Act—

(a) every primary school maintained by a local authority shall be managed by such local authority; and

(b) every maintained or assisted school other than a primary school maintained by a local authority shall be managed by a Board of Governors, or as the Minister may otherwise direct,

in accordance with this Act and any regulations made under this Act.

Primary Schools Maintained by Local Authorities

7. (1) The manager of every primary school maintained but not managed by a local authority before the commencement of this Act shall within six months of such commencement choose either—

(a) to transfer the management of the school to that local authority, which shall thereafter manage and maintain the school (hereinafter called a transferred school); or

(b) to continue to maintain the school as an unaided school.

(2) The manager shall notify his choice in writing to the local authority maintaining the school within six months after the commencement of this Act and the choice shall take effect on the 1st January next following.

(3) Where the management of a school is transferred to a local authority under this section, the service of any teacher in the establishment of the school immediately before and immediately after the transfer shall be deemed to be continuous service for the purpose of regulation 16 (1) of the Pensions Regulations.

8. (1) Where a transferred school was managed by a church, or an organization of churches, and it is the wish of the community served by the school that the religious traditions of the school should be respected, the former manager shall be appointed by the local authority to serve as the sponsor to the school.

(2) If the former manager, or any ten citizens belonging to the community served by the school, are aggrieved by the decision of a local authority to appoint, or to refuse to appoint, or to revoke the appointment of, the former manager as sponsor to the school, they may appeal in writing to the Minister, who shall make such inquiries as appear to him desirable or necessary, and whose decision shall be final.

(3) Where the former manager of a transferred school has been appointed by the local authority to serve as the sponsor to the school—

(a) the Teachers Service Commission, or any agent of the Teachers Service Commission responsible for the assignment of teachers to schools on behalf of the Teachers Service Commission, shall assign teachers to the school after consultation with and, so far as may be compatible with the maintenance of proper educational standards at the school and the economical use of public funds, with the agreement of the sponsor;

(b) the sponsor shall have the right to use the school buildings free of charge, when the buildings are not in use for school purposes, after giving reasonable notice of his intention to do so to the Headmaster of the school:

Provided that any additional expenses and the cost of making good any damage incurred during or in consequence of the sponsor using the buildings shall be defrayed by the sponsor; and

(c) religious instructions shall be given at the school in conformity with a syllabus prepared or approved under regulations made under section 19 of this Act after consultation with the sponsor.

(4) In determining what are the wishes of the community served by a school, the local authority or the Minister shall give due weight to the wishes of the parents of the children at the school.

9. (1) For every primary school maintained and managed by the local authority there shall be a school committee, established by the local authority, to advise the local authority on matters relating to the management of the school.

(2) The members of a school committee shall be appointed by the local authority in the prescribed number and manner, and the members of the committee shall include persons to represent the local authority, the community served by the school and, where a sponsor to the school has been appointed under section 8 of this Act, the sponsor.

Other Schools

10. (1) The Minister may, by order, establish a Board of Governors for any maintained or assisted school, other than a primary school managed and maintained by a local authority, or, if the manager of any unaided school applies to him, for that unaided school, and the Minister may—

(a) establish one Board of Governors for two or more schools; or

(b) establish Boards of Governors for two or more schools by means of the same order.

(2) The Minister may, by order, declare a Board of Governors to be a body corporate under the name of the Board of Governors of the school or schools, and such Board of Governors shall have perpetual succession and a common seal

with power to hold both movable and immovable property, and may in its corporate name sue and be sued.

(3) Where a Board of Governors is established, the Minister shall exercise all the functions of the Board during the interval of time that may elapse between the establishment of the Board and the first meeting of the Board.

11. An order establishing a Board of Governors shall provide for—

(a) the exercise by the Board of the duty of management of the school or schools, subject to this Act, the Teachers Service Commission Act 1966 and any regulations made under this Act and to any limitations or restrictions that may be imposed by the order;

(b) the membership of the Board, which shall be not less than five persons;

(c) including among the members of the Board representatives of the communities served by the school, of persons representing any voluntary body which was the founder of the school or its successor, and of any other persons or representatives of bodies or organizations that, in the opinion of the Minister, should be included;

(d) the appointment and resignation of members and the continuity of the membership of the Board;

(e) a person or persons representing the Minister to attend at meetings of the Board;

(f) in the case of a Board of Governors which is not a body corporate, vesting the movable and immovable property of the Board in trustees incorporated under any law or in the Public Trustee;

(h) any other matters which the Minister considers it necessary or desirable to provide for with respect to the status functions, constitution or procedure of the Board.

12. (1) Where in the opinion of the Minister, a Board of Governors has behaved irresponsibly or has failed to exercise properly its functions under this Act, he may in writing—

(a) suspend the Board from the exercise of and performance of all its powers and duties, and appoint an administrator to exercise and perform all the powers and duties of the Board for such period not exceeding one year as the Minister specifies;

(b) require the resignation of all or any of the members of the Board, and appoint or require the appointment of new members of the Board.

(2) The Minister shall make regulations providing for the manner in which an administrator appointed under subsection (1) of this section shall exercise all the powers and perform the duties of a Board of Governors.

Part IV — Registration of Unaided Schools

13. The Minister shall cause a register of unaided schools to be established and maintained, and the register shall be open to public inspection at all reasonable times.

14. (1) Any person who wishes to establish an unaided school shall first make application to the Minister for the school to be registered.

(2) An application for registration shall state the classification of the proposed school according to the prescribed nomenclature and the classes or forms to be provided in the school.

(3) In this section, "establish", in relation to a school, includes—

(a) providing any additional class or form not included in any previous registration; or

(b) providing any type of education not falling within the classification in which the school was previously registered; or

(c) changing ownership or management of the school; or

(d) transferring the school to a new site; or

(e) reopening a school that has been closed under section 16 of this Act.

15. (1) Where application is made for the registration of an unaided school, the Minister shall cause the school to be provisionally registered for a period of eighteen months, if he is satisfied that—

(a) the establishment of the school is consistent with the needs of Kenya and the economical and efficient provision of public education; and

(b) the premises and accommodation are suitable and adequate, having regard to the number, ages and sex of the pupils who are to attend the school, and fulfil the prescribed minimum requirements of health and safety and conform with any building regulations for the time being in force under any written law; and

(c) the manager is a suitable and proper person to be the manager of the school:

Provided that, where the establishment of the school consists only of one or more of the acts specified in paragraphs (a), (b), (c), (d) and (e) of section 14 (3) of this Act, the Minister may, in his discretion, register the school at the outset instead of first registering it provisionally.

(2) If, at the end of one year from the provisional registration of a school the Minister is satisfied that efficient and suitable instruction is being provided at the school, he may cause the school to be registered.

(3) The Minister may, as a condition of provisional registration or registration, require the manager of an unaided school to apply to him for an order establishing a Board of Governors for the school, and such a requirement may be made at any subsequent time.

(4) Where the Minister refuses to provisionally register or to register an unaided school, he shall inform the person making the application in writing of the grounds of refusal.

(5) All unaided schools which immediately before the commencement of this Act were registered under Part X of the Education Act (now repealed) shall be registered in the register forthwith upon such commencement.

16. (1) Where the Minister is satisfied that an unaided school which has been registered under this Part is objectionable because the school—

(a) fails to comply with paragraphs (a), (b) and (c) of section 15 (1) of this Act; or

(b) is a place in which efficient and suitable education or instruction is not being provided; or

(c) is being conducted or managed in a manner which is, in the opinion of the Minister, prejudicial to the physical, mental or moral welfare of the pupils of the school, or to peace, good order or good government in Kenya; or

(d) is a place in which a person is teaching who is not registered in the register of teachers kept under section 7 of the Teachers Service Commission Act 1966 and is not exempted under section 22 of that Act from registration; or

(e) fails to conform with regulations made under section 19 of this Act; or

(f) has not complied with a condition imposed under section 15 (3) of this Act,

the Minister may serve on the manager of the school a notice in writing specifying the respects in which the school is objectionable and requiring him to remedy the said matters within a specified period not exceeding six months:

Provided that if, in the opinion of the Minister, there are urgent reasons for the immediate closure of the school the Minister may order the manager of the school to close the school forthwith.

(2) If the manager of an unaided school fails to remedy the matters specified in a notice served on him under subsection (1) of this section within the period specified therein, the Minister shall order the manager to close the school.

(3) An unaided school which has been ordered to be closed under this section, and any unaided school which has remained closed for a period of six months or more, shall be removed from the register.

17. The Minister may make regulations with respect to registration of unaided schools and in particular such regulations may—

(a) prescribe the particulars to be entered in the register;

(b) prescribe the manner in which application for registration shall be made and the particulars, proof or evidence to be supplied by the applicant;

(c) prescribe with respect to any application for registration the procedure to be followed, the forms to be used and the fees to be paid;

(d) prescribe the conditions which may be attached to provisional registration, beyond that mentioned in section 15 (3) of this Act;

(e) provide for the issue, variation and revocation of certificates of provisional registration and certificates of registration;

(f) require the submission from time to time, or at any time, of any particulars, information, documents or returns by the manager of a registered unaided school;

(g) provide for any other matter that the Minister may consider necessary or desirable to provide for the purposes of this Part.

Part V — Inspection and Control of Schools

18. (1) The Minister shall appoint officers with authority to enter and inspect any school, or any place at which it is reasonably suspected that a school is being conducted, at any time, with or without notice, and to report to him with respect to the school or any aspect thereof.

(2) The Minister shall appoint officers with authority to enter any school at any time, with or without notice, and inspect or audit the accounts of the school or advise the manager of the school on the maintenance of accounting records, and may temporarily remove any books or records for the purpose of inspection or audit.

(3) On being so requested by an officer appointed under this section, the principal of the school shall place at the disposal of the officer all the facilities, records, accounts, notebooks, examination scripts and other materials belonging to the school that the officer may reasonably require for the purpose of the inspection of the school or the inspection or audit of its accounts.

(4) An officer inspecting a school under subsection (1) of this section shall have special regard to the maintenance of educational standards and to compliance with any regulations made under section 19 of this Act.

(5) In this section, "school" includes—

(a) any part of the school and any buildings used in connexion with the school, including workshops, dormitories, kitchens, sanatoria, hostels, ancillary buildings and any other buildings on the site of the school; and

(b) except in subsection (2) of this section, an institution or assembly for which a Minister other than the Minister is responsible.

19. The Minister may make regulations with respect to the conduct and management of schools and such regulations may—

(a) prescribe standards with regard to the numbers and qualifications of staff, the size of classes and the expenditure on educational materials;

(b) provide for the preparation or approval of curricula, syllabuses, books and other educational materials;

(c) prescribe minimum standards for the health and safety of pupils and for a satisfactory environment for education;

(d) provide for the keeping of registers and records and the submission of returns;

(e) provide for the admission, suspension, punishment and dismissal of pupils;

(f) prescribe the minimum number of days in a year on which instruction shall be given;

(g) prescribe how schools shall be classified and the name to be attached to each class of school;

(h) make different provision with respect to different classes or kinds of schools, impose conditions and make exceptions;

(i) provide for or prescribe such other matters as the Minister considers it necessary or desirable to provide for or prescribe.

Part VI – Examinations and Diplomas

20. (1) The Minister may provide for the conduct of public examinations, and may issue certificates or diplomas to pupils who have been successful in a public examination for the conduct of which he has provided.

(2) The Minister may issue certificates and diplomas to pupils who have successfully completed an approved course of education or training.

21. No person except—

(a) the persons and institutions named in the Second Schedule of this Act; or

(b) a person who has received the consent of the Minister, given by notice in the Gazette,

shall issue a certificate or diploma to any person indicating, or purporting to indicate, that a person has successfully completed a course of education or training, or has attained a particular educational standard, or possesses any skill, knowledge or professional competence.

22. The Minister may make regulations—

(a) prescribing the manner in which certificates or diplomas may be issued under section 20 of this Act;

(b) prescribing the manner in which public examinations shall be conducted, and the conditions of entry and the fees to be charged;

(c) concerning the submission of applications for the Minister's consent to the issue of certificates and diplomas, and the revocation of such consent.

Part VII – The Kenya Institute of Education

23. (1) There is hereby established the Kenya Institute of Education with responsibility for the co-ordination of institutions devoted to the training of teachers, the conduct of examinations to enable persons to become qualified teachers, the conduct and promotion of educational research, the preparation of educational materials and other matters connected with the training of teachers and the development of education and training.

(2) The Minister may, by order, prescribe—

(a) the duties, powers and functions of the Institute;

(b) the manner in which the Institute shall be managed and controlled by a Council including persons representing the Minister, the University College, Nairobi and the maintained training colleges of Kenya;

(c) the constitution, duties, powers and functions of an Academic Board responsible to the Council for the academic management of the Institute;

(d) that the movable and immovable property of the Institute may be vested in the Public Trustee and the manner in which they shall be so vested; and

(e) any other matters with respect to the conduct and management of the Institute which the Minister considers it necessary or desirable to provide for.

Part VIII — Miscellaneous

24. The Minister may, at the request of any local authority or otherwise, by notice in the Gazette, prescribe the area to be served by a public school.

25. The Minister, or the manager of a school, may require any person attending the school, or applying for admission to the school, to undergo medical examination by a medical practitioner.

26. (1) If the parent of a pupil at a public school requests that the pupil be wholly or partly excused from attending religious worship, or religious worship and religious instruction, in the school, the pupil shall be excused such attendance until the request is withdrawn.

(2) Where the parent of a pupil at a public school wishes the pupil to attend religous worship or religious instruction of a kind which is not provided in the school, the school shall provide such facilities as may be practicable for the pupil to receive religious instruction and attend religious worship of the kind desired by the parent.

27. (1) Where the Minister is satisfied, upon complaint made by any person or otherwise, that a local authority, or the Board of Governors or manager of any school, or a sponsor, or the Institute, or the Teachers Service Commission, has acted or is proposing to act unreasonably or in contravention of the policy of the Government with respect to education as approved from time to time in Parliament, in the exercise of any functions entrusted to it by or under this Act, or the Teachers Service Commission Act 1966, he may give such directions as to the exercise of such functions as appear to him expedient.

(2) Where the Minister is satisfied that a local authority, or the Board of Governors or manager of any school, or the Institute, or the Teachers Service Commission established as aforesaid, has failed to discharge any duty imposed upon it by, or for the purposes of, this Act, or the Teachers Service Commission

Act 1966, he may give such directions as may be necessary for securing compliance with this Act or the Teachers Service Commission Act 1966:

Provided that, where the estimates of expenditure to be incurred by any local authority in the performance of any function entrusted to it under section 5 of this Act are subject to the approval of the Minister for the time being responsible for local government under Part XV of the Local Government Regulations 1963, any direction given under this subsection to a local authority shall be subject to the agreement of the Minister for the time being responsible for local government.

Part IX — Financial

28. (1) The Minister may from time to time from public funds—

(a) establish, maintain, assist, make grants-in-aid of or make advances on loan in respect of—

(i) schools;

(ii) establishments or provision for the boarding or feeding of pupils;

(iii) organizations or establishments responsible for educational development or research, or the promotion or co-ordination of education, or the welfare of students;

(iv) organizations responsible for the conduct of public examinations;

(b) make grants-in-aid to any institution of higher education;

(c) provide for the conduct of such public examinations as are held under the supervision or control of the Ministry;

(d) make grants-in-aid to local authorities for the purpose of any functions entrusted to them under section 5 of this Act;

(e) provide in whole or in part for the transport of pupils to or from any public school;

(f) provide for the medical inspection of pupils;

(g) provide scholarships or bursaries to assist in the education, maintenance and transport of pupils who are undergoing, or proceeding to, or returning from courses of instruction at an institution approved by the Minister;

(h) provide for the reimbursement of the expenses of any body constituted under this Act;

(i) provide for, or make grants in aid of, educational conferences, exhibitions, displays, dramatic or film presentations, sports or other occasions of an educational character or purpose;

(j) make such other provision for the carrying on of education as may be consistent with this Act.

(2) Grants-in-aid may be made for either capital or recurrent purposes.

29. The Minister may make regulations prescribing—

(a) the conditions upon which grants which may lawfully be made out of public funds for the maintenance or assistance of schools, organizations or establishments may be made;

(b) the fees to be charged or remitted at any school which received a grant out of public funds, and the liability of parents for the payment of such fees;

(c) the manner in which scholarships or bursaries may be granted, increased, reduced or withdrawn;

(d) the manner in which and the conditions under which grants are made to any institution of higher education;

(e) any other matter with respect to public funds relating to the submission of estimates, the maintenance and submission of accounting records, the use to which grants may be applied and the disposal of surpluses and reserve funds.

30. Any person who—

(a) establishes, manages, maintains or conducts an unaided school which has not been provisionally registered or registered, or whose provisional registration has expired, or which has been removed from the register in accordance with section 16 (3) of this Act; or

(b) issues a certificate or diploma contrary to section 20 (1) of this Act; or

(c) hinders or obstructs any officer of the Ministry acting in the course of his duty as such, or any person exercising any powers, or performing any duties, conferred or imposed by or under this Act,

shall be guilty of an offence and liable to a fine not exceeding five thousand shillings or to imprisonment for a term not exceeding six months, or to both such fine and such imprisonment.

31. Without prejudice to the other provisions in this Act for the making of regulations for particular purposes, the Minister may make regulations generally for the better carrying out of the purposes of this Act.

32. The Education Act is repealed:

Provided that the following Orders made under that Act, namely—

(a) the Education (Hospital Hill School Governors) Order;

(b) the Education (Boards of Governors) Order 1964;

(c) the Kenya Polytechnic (Board of Governors) Order 1965; and

(d) the Mombasa Technical Institute (Board of Governors) Order 1966,

shall continue in force as though made under this Act, and accordingly the Boards of Governors established by those Orders shall upon the commencement of this Act—

(i) be deemed to have been established and incorporated under section 10 of this Act; and

(ii) hold the same property and be subject to the same obligations as they held or were subject to immediately before such commencement.

Notes

INTRODUCTION

1. Guy Hunter, *Manpower, Employment and Education in the Rural Economy of Tanzania,* African Research Monographs No. 9 (Paris: UNESCO, International Institute for Educational Planning, 1966) p. 12.
2. Simon Ottenberg, "The Social and Administrative History of a Nigerian Township," *International Journal of Comparative Sociology,* VII, 1, 193.
3. Simon Ottenberg, "Local Government and the Law in Southern Nigeria," ibid., 2, 1–2, 33.

CHAPTER I

1. *Report of the Commission Appointed to Enquire into and Report on the Financial Position and System of Taxation in Kenya* (London: HMSO, 1936), pp. 168–169.
2. Nairobi: Government Printer, 1948.
3. The history of the movement is conveniently summarized in Carl G. Rosberg and J. Nottingham, *The Myth of Mau Mau* (New York: Praeger, 1966), pp. 125–131.
4. An account of one of these schools may be found in Mbiyu Koinange, *The People of Kenya Speak for Themselves* (Detroit: Kenya Publishers Fund, 1955), pp. 25 ff.
5. Education Department, *Annual Report, 1937* (Nairobi: Government Printer, 1937), p. 67.
6. The Beecher Report, *African Education in Kenya* (Nairobi: Government Printer, 1949), p. 27.
7. Ibid., pp. 32–33.
8. Oginga Odinga, *Not Yet Uhuru* (New York: Hill & Wang, 1967), p. 52.
9. Cf. the discussion in the legislature on the Education Act of 1968 in the National Assembly, *Official Report,* 15 and 16 January 1968.
10. Education Department, *Annual Report, 1928* (Nairobi: Government Printer, 1928), p. 57.
11. Education Department, *Annual Report, 1929* (Nairobi: Government Printer, 1929), p. 8.
12. The Beecher Report, p. 101.
13. Education Department, *Annual Summary, 1955* (Nairobi: Government Printer, 1955), p. 18.
14. *Journal of African Administration,* XII, 3 (July 1960), 148.
15. D. A. Lury and A. A. Shah, *Local Government in Kenya, Expenditure and Income 1959–1961,* Reprint Series No. 15 (Nairobi: Institute for Development Studies, n.d.), pp. 8–9.
16. *Journal of African Administration,* loc. cit.
17. See below, pp. 15–18, 19–21.
18. Constitution of Kenya, Schedule 1 (*Kenya Gazette* Supplement No. 105, December 10, 1963).
19. Legal Notice No. 74 (1965).

CHAPTER II

1. Hereinafter, PEO, CEO, and AEO respectively.
2. The National Assembly, *Official Report,* 11 January 1958, col. 4033.
3. An amusing and revealing account of a headmaster's travails in fee collection can be found in the *Kenya Teacher,* June 1967, pp. 15–16.
4. The National Assembly, *Official Report,* 9 January 1968, col. 3881.
5. Cf. the further discussion of fees as part of the council's revenue in Chapter III following, pp. 38–39, 40.
6. Legal Notice No. 256 (1963), Sec. 91.
7. Cf. Chapter III following, pp. 46–51.
8. Teachers Service Commission Act, 1966 (No. 2 of 1967), Sec. 4 (1) (a) (b).
9. Cf., for example, the reply in answer to a member's question in the National Assembly, *Official Report,* 24 October 1967, cols. 1072–1073.
10. *Development Plan, 1966–1970* (Nairobi: Government Printer, 1966), p. 310.
11. Kenya Education Commission, *Report* (Nairobi: Government Printer, 1965), Part II, paras. 532 ff.
12. Cf. the comments on the cost of universal primary education in Chapter III following, pp. 51–58.
13. *East African Standard,* 28 April 1967.
14. Cf. the discussion of the cost of universal primary education below, pp. 51–58.
15. The National Assembly, *Official Report,* 7 December 1967, col. 3041 (Mr. Oduya).
16. Kenya Education Commission, *Report,* Part II, para. 550.
17. Ministry of Education, *Annual Summary, 1965* (Nairobi: Government Printer, 1965), p. 21, and *Triennial Survey, 1966* (Nairobi: Government Printer, 1966), p. 69. The Education Commission uses a figure of 1,034,000 for 1965 (*Annual Summary, 1965,* p. 6).
18. Cf. the figures shown in the Kenya Education Commission, *Report.* Part II, para. 561, Table IX. Note that these figures would appear to be on the optimistic side; the figure of 137.3 percent in Nairobi is accounted for by the fact that large numbers of children not residing permanently in the city attend school there.
19. Kenya Education Commission, *Report,* Part II, para. 562.
20. Ibid.
21. I am indebted to Dr. Lewis Brownstein for much of the information in these paragraphs. His detailed study on school leavers in selected areas of Kenya is forthcoming.
22. Cf. Christian Council of Kenya, "After School, What?" mimeographed (Nairobi, 1966).
23. The National Assembly, *Official Report,* 11 January 1968, cols. 4007–4008.
24. Kenya Education Commission, *Report,* Part I, para. 110.
25. "After School, What?" p. 69.
26. This type of project is discussed in detail in ibid., pp. 60–65.

CHAPTER III

1. Excludes £ 414,700 of direct appropriations in aid from the Ministry of Education.
2. The latter factor is being altered through the introduction of a formula system of central bloc grants in 1968.
3. For details of the GPT collection process, cf. the Graduated Personal Tax Act (No. 38 of 1966).

4. Recent changes in the Graduated Personal Tax Act will solve this problem in part through having 50 percent of the GPT collected in Nairobi turned over to the Ministry of Local Government for redistribution to the counties.

5. Nairobi: East Africa Publishing House, 1968.

6. Ministry of Education, "Constraint and Strategy in Planning Education," mimeographed (Kericho, Kenya: Conference on Education, Employment, and Rural Development, 1966), p. 10.

7. Public Salaries Review Commission, *Report* (Nairobi: Government Printer, 1967), para. 336.

8. Kenya Education Commission, *Report* (Nairobi: Government Printer, 1965), Part II, para. 547.

9. Ministry of Education, "Constraint and Strategy in Planning Education," p. 10.

10. Kenya Education Commission, *Report,* Part II, para. 549.

11. Public Salaries Review Commission, *Report,* para. 328.

12. The National Assembly, *Official Report,* 7 December 1967, cols. 3026–3028.

13. Ibid., cols. 3030–3031.

14. Ibid., col. 3033.

15. Ibid., col. 3047.

16. Ibid.

17. Public Salaries Review Commission, *Report,* para. 330.

18. Ibid., para. 339.

19. The National Assembly, *Official Report,* 7 December 1967, col. 2872.

20. Sessional Paper No. 11 (1967), para. 13.

21. A. Calloway and A. Musone, *Financing of Education in Nigeria,* African Research Monographs No. 15 (Paris: UNESCO, International Institute for Educational Planning, 1968), pp. 36 ff.

22. Kenya Education Commission, *Report,* Part II, para. 564.

23. Ibid., para. 566.

24. The National Assembly, *Official Report,* 9 January 1968, col. 3874.

25. Ibid., 11 January 1968, col. 4007. Cf., for example, the comments of opposition members.

CHAPTER IV

1. The National Assembly, *Official Report,* 8 January 1968, col. 3810.

2. Ibid., col. 3811.

3. Education Act of 1968 (No. 5 of 1968). The text of the act is reproduced in the appendix to this volume (pp. 89–101).

4. The National Assembly, *Official Report,* 8 January 1968, col. 3822.

5. Legal Notice No. 105 (replacing Legal Notice No. 74 [1965]).

6. The National Assembly, *Official Report,* 9 January 1968, col. 3871.

7. The term "sponsor" is discussed below, pp. 65, 66–68, and 70. The Local Government Regulations (Sec. 91) permitted appointment of nonmembers to any council committee, requiring only that two-thirds of the members be councilors but allowing the local authority to determine the total number on any committee.

8. The National Assembly, *Official Report,* 9 January 1968, cols. 3879–3880.

9. The Education (School Committee) Regulations (1968), Legal Notice No. 104.

10. *Development Estimates, 1967/68* (Nairobi: Government Printer, 1967), pp. 42–43.

11. Education Act of 1968, Sec. 15 (1) (a).

12. The National Assembly, *Official Report,* 8 January 1968, col. 3812.

106

13. Ibid., 11 January 1968, cols. 4045–4046.
14. Ibid., 8 January 1968, col. 3812.
15. Ibid., 11 January 1968, col. 4019–4020.
16. Ibid., col. 4033.
17. Ibid., 15 January 1968, col. 4161.
18. Ibid., 11 January 1968, cols. 4013–4014.
19. Ibid., 15 January 1968, col. 4148.

CONCLUSION

1. Jon Moris, "Education and Training of the Farmer," mimeographed (Kericho, Kenya: Conference on Education, Employment, and Rural Development, 1966), p. D1.
2. Francis X. Sutton, "Aid and the Problems of Education, Employment and Rural Development," mimeographed (Kericho, Kenya: Conference on Education, Employment, and Rural Development, 1966), p. 9.
3. Philip Foster, *Education and Social Change in Ghana* (Chicago: Univ. of Chicago Press, 1965), pp. 162 ff.
4. Fergus B. Wilson, *Man_____ _____ning,* Fundamentals of Educational Planning S_____ Institute for Educational Planning, n.d.), p. 199.

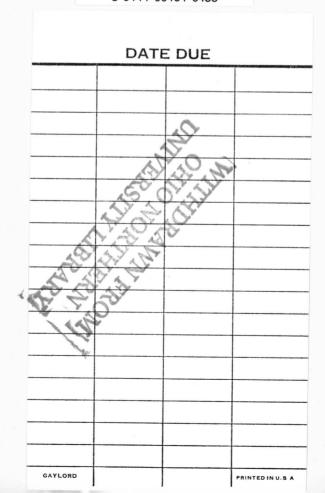

DATE DUE

GAYLORD   PRINTED IN U.S.A